Historic Tales
of
MACOMB COUNTY

Historic Tales
— *of* —
MACOMB COUNTY

BARB PERT TEMPLETON

THE
History
PRESS

Published by The History Press
Charleston, SC
www.historypress.com

First published 2020

Manufactured in the United States

ISBN 9781467145251

Library of Congress Control Number: 2020932096

For Mom and my David

Contents

CONTENTS

Preface

S tories. We all have our own, and really, no two are the same. I've been interested in talking to people and telling their tales for decades and have done so as a reporter and freelance writer in Macomb County since 1987. Yet despite that extremely large cache of stories—there's always more to share.

This book has historic notes and tales from the past, but they are presented in a unique way, featuring the people who lived them and made them happen. We include personal stories of politicians, inventors, soldiers and farmers, a circus family and several librarians who played a part in making Macomb County prosper.

You might ask, where is Macomb County and what makes it interesting? Well, it's an area in eastern Michigan that's considered part of metro Detroit and includes twenty-seven villages, cities and townships that boast the fifth-largest population in the state. The county covers 479 miles, of which 92 are under water in the form of Lake St. Clair. The county was founded in 1818 and named after War of 1812 veteran Alexander Macomb Jr. Mount Clemens is the county seat. Today, it has a county executive form of government.

Acknowledgements

*B*eing adjacent to the Motor City and Motown makes Macomb County a great place to call home. Sure, we have our fair share of celebrities, but it's actually the lives of the ordinary people who did extraordinary things here over the last two hundred years that are exciting to discover.

Speaking of people, completing this book required lots of those, too, including:

Ruth Koppinger Suwalkowski: My good friend who seemed to know I should write this book before I did. For providing endless support, lots of bull sessions via Facebook private messenger, stories and photos of her hometown, Memphis, and just a straight-up cheerleader day or night during this hectic process.

Pat Hallman, of Shelby Township, a walking, talking rolodex of all things historical in much of Macomb County. She answered my calls, did her best to provide information or point me in the right direction and emailed any relevant documents or photos that might be useful.

Alan Naldrett, a Chesterfield Township author several times over with Arcadia Press, who was always an email away with tips, advice and positive vibes when the going got tough.

Wayne Oehmke, leading the way for me with contacts for Macomb Township, including introducing me to his childhood friend Shelley Stier Henshaw. She, in turn, invited me into her home to look at photos and hear her stories of growing up in the township although we were total strangers.

Acknowledgements

Mayor Suzanne Pixley, another Arcadia author from East Pointe, also offered ideas about how to find photos, how to catalogue them and, possibly the best advice of all, how to get some sleep and go on a cruise, once the book was done.

Adam Mueller, adult services librarian at the Chesterfield Township Library, who came through big time with not only information about the late George Furton but he also shared his own just published book on Bernard Trinity with me and sent along photos for both subjects without delay.

1

Bruce Township

Founded in 1833, Bruce Township roots go all the way back to the original formation of Macomb County. As Bruce Township is primarily a farming community, livestock has always been an important agricultural part of community life. Despite the reduction in farming, today much of the township's thirty-six square miles remains open space. Bruce Township has the distinction of being the highest point in Macomb County at 1,150 feet, in an area once known as Trombley Mountain. The mountain was atop a 4,000-acre farm, where 5,500 head of cattle used to roam. The land was sold to Michigan Ford Proving Grounds, which used it for testing Ford trucks and cars. Much of the Village of Romeo is located within the township.

JUDGE NEIL EDWIN REID

Court Stenographer to Supreme Court Justice

Michigan's second Supreme Court justice, Neil Reid, was born in 1871 in Bruce Township and had a stellar career spanning more than sixty years, a state record at that time. Described as six-foot-four and gaunt, yet colorful, Reid had a reputation for being a tough judge, especially with cases regarding prohibition violators and armed robbers.

Reid attended high schools in Romeo and Almont, went on to Harvard University for one year, where he learned shorthand, and was a store clerk and part-time court reporter. He began working as a court stenographer in Mount Clemens in 1894 and obtained his law degree in 1896 from the Detroit College of Law. He was admitted to practice that same year.

He married Maude C. Rowley of Mount Clemens on January 4, 1900; they had no children.

Governor Fred W. Warner appointed Reid, a Republican, as a Macomb County Probate Court judge in 1910, and he served for thirteen years. He then became a Macomb Circuit Court judge, a position he held for two ten-year terms.

While a Macomb Circuit Court judge, Reid was involved in a notorious case out of Memphis, Michigan, involving the Memphis State Bank. In 1928, Reid sentenced Stanley Kolasinski and Harry Lasky after they were convicted of stealing $7,000 during a bank robbery based on the testimony of bank cashier Henry M. Brown. In 1932, Brown, along with his wife, committed suicide and left a note confessing to embezzling money from the bank over several years. Kolasinski was ordered released from Jackson State Prison, and Lasky's remaining parole was dismissed. An audit of the bank found over $4,000 unaccounted for, and the bank closed.

Neil Edwin Reid set a state record for longevity in service to the court system. Judge Reid was born in Bruce Township, Michigan, on April 24, 1871. This portrait is from 1950. *From the Macomb Daily.*

In another interesting case, Reid allowed an eighteen-year-old man three weeks to decide if he would "go straight" and avoid a stint in jail after he pleaded guilty to stealing $365 from his stepmother in Warren in 1932. Then there was the man known as the "human fly" who was convicted of breaking into a Tobacco Company warehouse in Detroit and was sentenced to ten to fifteen years in prison. Reid had offered leniency to the thief if he would divulge the name of his accomplice. The defendant refused and was sent to Michigan State Prison in Jackson.

Reid actually found himself in the defendant's chair, not the jurist, when he breached the gaming laws in northern Michigan in 1919. The deer season was still hours away when Reid took down a fine buck in Hancock; he was fined $50 plus $16 in court costs. He also had to surrender his Remington rifle, and the deer was donated to feed families in the local indigent home.

In 1944, Reid won his first election to the Michigan Supreme Court, defeating incumbent Bert Chandler. His campaign was deemed a "postcard" race in that he sent all his friends postcards requesting their votes. Reid credited his friends for the victory. He was named the court's chief judge in 1951.

Beyond the courtroom, Reid was active with the local Masons and Boy Scouts and enjoyed fishing and hunting. In 1956, the eighty-five-year-old Reid died in office.

Reid's last will was unusual, as it had been written in longhand in 1918, thirty-eight years prior to his passing. All but $2,000 of the estate, left for his brother James, who had already passed away, was bequeathed to his widow, Maude. It was reported that Reid held $25,000 in stocks and bonds in a safety deposit box, but there was no deed for some seven thousand acres of property he owned.

2

Chesterfield Township

*C*hesterfield Township, founded in 1842, was mainly a farming community and initially bore such monikers as Milton, Hart and Slipper Corner. Residents finally decided on Chesterfield after an English nobleman whose title was Lord Chesterfield. The township is particularly unique, as it has property off Sugarbush and Cotton Roads that is five to ten thousand years old and was an Indian settlement and burial ground known as the Old Indian Trail Road. When the Grand Trunk Railroad came through in 1865, businesses were established. A general law township, Chesterfield didn't become a charter township until 1989. Today, the township thrives with homes and businesses and covers 30.7 square miles. It has its own police and fire departments that provide services to some forty-four thousand residents.

DEAN NALDRETT

A Charming Pioneer for Education

As superintendent of Anchor Bay Schools in the 1950s, Dean Naldrett was right in the thick of the small country school districts merging into one big school district, and the road to change was rough. Verbal fights at local school board meetings where the police had to be called to restore order were becoming the norm, and Naldrett was right out front trying to ease the battle.

When he suddenly died at the age of forty-two, just a few years into his leadership role in the rural school district, the shock and dismay were palpable in the community—so was admiration for a man who crammed three lifetimes into one, leaving behind an amazing legacy.

Naldrett was born on a farm in Ithaca, Michigan, in 1916. His parents, Allen and Bertha (Jessup) Naldrett, raised horses and cattle along with bean and corn crops on land purchased by his grandfather, who immigrated from Sussex County, England, at the turn of the century. Dean enjoyed the small-town farm life and was an avid fan of the new national sport, baseball. Still, farming was not for Naldrett, and after graduating from high school in 1936, he enrolled in the education program at Central Michigan University in Mt. Pleasant, Michigan. While mainly studying science and mathematics, he was also active in on campus athletics.

He met his wife, Ilah M. Cole, at Central Michigan, and they were married in 1941. Naldrett went on to serve as a lieutenant commander in the navy during World War II and the Korean War.

After returning home to a principal's post in Chesterfield Township, he was named superintendent of the school district. The school systems in the

The Naldrett family, pictured here in 1957 (*from left to right*): Phyllis (Maddix), mother Ilah with Ronald on her lap, Sherrell (Hissong) and Dean with Alan on his lap. *Courtesy of the Naldrett family.*

Dean Naldrett. *Courtesy of the Naldrett family.*

area were changing, as many people, especially Naldrett, felt it was time that the many rural schools in the area were absorbed into larger districts better equipped to meet the evolving educational needs of the students.

Naldrett's devotion to the plan payed off, and in 1955, the name of the newly transformed and hard-fought-for district became Anchor Bay School District.

By then the father of four children—Phyllis, Sherrell, Alan and Ronald—Naldrett had a charming personality and was known around the house as a practical joker. On April Fool's Day, his family would find sugar in the saltshaker and clocks set back an hour. At a wedding reception, he jumped into the car with the bride and drove off with her, surprising her new husband. Favorite family outings included going hunting and playing baseball.

He was also very active in many organizations, including the National and Michigan Education Associations, the Macomb County Association of School Superintendents, the First Congregational Church of New Baltimore and the Rotary Club. He continued to love baseball and helped form (in the New Baltimore area) the Babe Ruth League for older boys and Little League for younger ones, encouraging the groups to use school-owned baseball fields. He also encouraged athletics at Anchor Bay Schools and helped organize the football, track, baseball and girls' and boys' basketball teams.

In September 1958, he went to a convention for the Michigan School Administrators Association Meeting on Mackinac Island. Ironically, on the way there, he arranged for the new polio vaccine to be sent to Anchor Bay Schools. While at the convention, he was stricken with what was thought to be Asian flu. The superintendent of Ithaca Schools took him to his parents' house in Ithaca. Naldrett worsened and was taken to Alma Community Hospital, where he was placed in an iron lung, but he died three days later on September 22, 1958. An autopsy revealed that Dean Naldrett had unknowingly contracted the bulbar polio virus. Naldrett was the only one in his family who had not had Salk anti-polio shots. It was later determined that he had likely contracted the polio from one of his baseball players.

Dean's funeral in Ithaca caused Anchor Bay Schools (and St. Mary's Catholic) to be closed. Many busloads of the townspeople (including students) took the three-hour trip to Ithaca from Chesterfield Township and the nearby city of New Baltimore. Many others drove their own cars. The unprecedented crowd exhibited a level of appreciation rarely experienced in either small town. The *Detroit Free Press* had a banner headline on the second front page proclaiming, "Town Closes to Honor Son."

Two years later, in 1960, the Anchor Bay School Board voted to name the second elementary school in the school system after Naldrett. The school, whose student body was made up of children from Selfridge Air Force Base, brought a level of diversity to the surrounding communities that Naldrett would have been proud of.

After his death, his widow, Ilah, continued to teach at Anchor Bay Elementary School for over twenty years, in the process helping to create the first "Readiness Room" for children who need a little more attention before entering the first grade.

Loved not only for his charm and wit, Dean Naldrett was also the first superintendent of the consolidated Anchor Bay School District and instrumental in ushering in the modern age of education to the Anchor Bay area, presiding over the end of the little red schoolhouse days.

Additionally, Naldrett helped save the one-room Big Stone School from destruction by requesting it be moved to the back of the high school to be used as a storage facility. There it remained for many years, until 1990, when a Big Stone School Committee was formed and restored the school, moving it to a more accessible part of the school grounds.

BERNARD AND CEOLA TRINITY

A Neighborhood Library at Home

In 1948, when Bernard and Ceola Trinity discovered a three-acre parcel of land for sale at Cotton and Sugarbush Roads in Chesterfield Township, it happened quite by accident. The young couple, who were married in Detroit in 1946, were on a picnic chatting about moving to the country when a for sale sign lured them to the acreage. They soon moved to the property, constructing an 1,800-square-foot home to raise their children, Phillip Michael and Carol Lynn.

Bernard Trinity, who had previously worked at Chrysler while attending college, only to have his studies interrupted by a five-year stint in the U.S. Army Medical Corps, decided the factory life in the city wasn't for him. A

Bernard and Ceola Trinity. *Trinity History Collection, Chesterfield Township Library.*

rural setting where he could be creative was a better fit, and his true calling was to be a craftsman, so he quickly taught himself to work with leather and upholstery. An avid reader, he also enjoyed collecting books and soon had a home library with over five hundred titles.

When word began to spread that the Trinitys had a miniature library in their home, people started to pop in and ask if they could borrow something from the collection. Pretty soon, the steady footsteps of both children and adults in pursuit of a good book led Trinity to move the setup from his home to his nearby upholstery shop. An article in a 1955 issue of the local newspaper described it as a fourteen-by-eighteen-foot pine-paneled room.

At times known as the "Neighborhood Library" or the "Trinity Library," the collection grew as books borrowed from the county library or simply donated began to fill the shelves. Still, make no mistake, this venture remained a simple grass-roots effort with no library cards or computerized card catalogues; in fact, all books were borrowed on the honor system. On the first anniversary of the library's opening in May 1956, Bernard Trinity

Bernard Trinity talking to students in the library. *Trinity History Collection, Chesterfield Township Library.*

reported that seventy-one patrons had borrowed five hundred books and all but one item were returned undamaged.

Within two years, the Trinity Library became part of the Macomb County Library System, and all the books were organized to make it a formal branch. This was a big boost that not only provided county financial support for the little neighborhood library but also led to a renovation project the next year that increased the size from 252 square feet to 780 square feet. The new facility, still located in the yard on the Trinity family property, now had a children's room complete with a fireplace so story time would be cozy.

Despite the more modern adjustments to the book catalogue and library space, the atmosphere remained rustic, and historic artifacts from the Trinity family's personal collection began to appear around the library. Amid an ever-growing collection of books, visitors could observe old butter churns, a spinning wheel and, at one point, a cuckoo clock that had been donated by the Ladies Auxiliary of the Chesterfield Fire Department.

The Neighborhood Library also became a welcoming place for student field trips and the gathering of local clubs and organizations. At one point in the late 1950s, a group of archaeology students from Wayne State University used the library as base camp as they surveyed the Sugarbush area seeking Native American artifacts.

Bernard and Ceolo Trinity took courses and gained state certification as librarians in order to maintain the library. They were assisted by a student librarian from the high school and dozens of volunteers. In 1965, the Trinity Library was referred to as the only private public library in the state, one that managed to circulate twelve thousand books annually.

Along the way, Bernard Trinity's lifelong love of history grew into a collection of more than one thousand antiques. He and his wife were appointed the official Chesterfield Township historians, and soon the Trinity Museum sprang up next to the Neighborhood Library. The one-room museum was constructed to include a penny candy store, both general and hardware stores and a miniature post office with letters dating to 1885. A special touch for children during the holiday season included a 1907 vintage crank phone that served as hotline to Santa and Mrs. Claus at the North Pole. Bernard Trinity told a local newspaper at the time that if the White House and the Kremlin could have hotlines, kids ought to have one too. Admission to the museum was free.

It seemed 1968 was a banner year for Bernard. He was formally honored by the Michigan House of Representatives with a resolution recognizing the Trinity Historical Museum. Then the Macomb County Historical Society created an award of merit and appreciation naming Bernard as its first recipient and the Southeastern Michigan Tourist Association selected him as a director.

The library made the local newspaper for another reason in 1968 when Bernard declared, "We want our Ding-Dong back," after it was stolen from

Bernard Trinity in the Trinity Historical Museum. *Trinity History Collection, Chesterfield Township Library.*

out in front of the museum. Taking the bell was quite a feat, as it weighed over three hundred pounds. He would often ring it for visitors, and its sound could be heard a mile away. There's no record of whether or not the bell was ever recovered.

By the early 1970s, the library was in jeopardy: the county decided to no longer fund the small Chesterfield Township branch. Supporters sought approval on the November 1972 ballot of a .5 millage to fund the operation of the library. Bernard Trinity stood out at the polls in the pouring rain promoting the proposal, but it failed. The library had only sought $12,000 annually, which would cover a salary and operations, to stay open.

Just as it seemed the beloved local library would have to close, the township stepped in and agreed to finance the branch. By 1990, there was nearly $40,000 in the township budget earmarked for the little library, which now housed 7,500 books. When Bernard Trinity suddenly passed away in 1976 at the age of fifty-nine, the library and museum were left to Ceola Trinity to run, and she did just that until her retirement in 1991.

GEORGE FURTON

The Man of Many "Hats"

The average size of a newborn baby is between five and eight pounds, so when George Clement Furton bounced into the world in October 1923 weighing over eleven pounds, perhaps it was a sign of the big life he would lead.

He was born at the home of his grandparents off Main Street in New Baltimore, the first child of Joseph and Odessa (Rivard) Furton. He grew up on a farm off Sugarbush Road in Chesterfield Township, where his father raised chickens and hogs in addition to a large vegetable garden surrounded by apple and cherry trees on the property. The family's small but sturdy old home housed Furton, his parents and two younger brothers but lacked indoor plumbing.

In a book he penned himself to share his life story, Furton describes an average childhood for the period: food was plentiful on the farm, but money was scarce—shoes were filled with cardboard bottoms. He enjoyed eighth-grade graduation from the Green School along with nine other pupils and went onto Mount Clemens High School to complete his education. A memorable and nearly tragic incident Furton recalled from his time riding the school bus was the day he stepped off and in front of the bus and it

President George Bush with George Furton. *Trinity History Collection, Chesterfield Township Library.*

ran him over. Fortunately, he landed between the wheels and survived the mishap with a simple bump on his head.

Furton also survived three years in the army serving overseas during World War II. When he returned stateside, he went straight home to Chesterfield Township and reunited with his wife, Gerry, and one-year-old daughter, Dianne, whose birth and first year of life he had missed.

Employed at various collision and bump shops in his twenties, Furton grew fond of repairing and restoring cars totaled in wrecks and took pride in seeing old Cadillac convertibles returned to the roadways thanks to his handiwork. He also began what would be a lifelong stint as a local public servant. In 1954, the township board wanted to start a volunteer fire department and soon welcomed a roster of local men who attended sixteen weeks of training before establishing the department. Furton was named the first assistant fire chief and later the chief, earning just fifty dollars a year for the head title. At one point, he asked the township supervisor for a fifty dollar a year raise just to cover the cost of clothes ruined in service and was

George Furton campaigning for state representative. *Trinity Historical Collection, Chesterfield Township.*

denied. His fellow firefighters paid a call on the supervisor one day when he was in his barn milking his cows, as they didn't want to lose their chief. The pay increase was granted, and Furton stayed on for a total of nine years.

The chief's role was the launching pad for Furton's decades of service to the township. After working at the Tech Center in Warren and getting divorced, he opened his own real estate business in Chesterfield and began serving on many local nonprofit boards. In addition to being a charter member of the Chesterfield Township Historical Society, Furton belonged to the American Legion, the Veterans of Foreign Wars and the Lions Club.

Lifelong friend Ron Rose described Furton this way:

> *I have watched George throughout the years and know him as a man who will extend himself for others in need, even strangers. He is a man who would say and do what is right, always. He is an idea man, a thinker, a source of seemingly endless energy that all of us could emulate.*

The public arena drew Furton in when he was elected to a two-year term in the state House of Representatives, representing the Seventy-Fifth District. He followed that up with two four-year terms as treasurer of Chesterfield Township, serving from 1988 to 1996. In fact, he launched a write-in campaign after being ousted from an August primary ballot in 1996 by challenger Ray Novak, whom Furton said victimized him with "dirty politics," according to a local newspaper. Feeling he lost at the ballot box because of an anonymous political mailer to voters that reported he had not stuck to his campaign promises, Furton and many supporters launched the write-in campaign. He wanted to ensure his good reputation survived, and his constituents were assured he wasn't "a crook who didn't do his job." Despite his passionate defense, the write-in campaign was not successful, and his time as a politician ended.

As a founding member of the Chesterfield Business Association, Furton remained active with his real estate business over the years and was named Macomb County Realtor of the Year in 1979. In his book, Furton stated that he made many home sales and lots of money and enjoyed spending it on Buicks, cigars, booze and parties.

He was also always a man on the go in terms of transportation. He learned to pilot a plane in the late 1940s and went on to serve in the Civil Air Patrol and the U.S. Air Force's civilian auxiliary for many years. Furton also purchased his own plane and piloted it for some thirty years, enjoying private trips around the country. Motorcycles also captured his attention for periods of time, but perhaps his most treasured vehicle was a Model T.

He had actually acquired his first 1924 Model T when he was just thirteen years old. It had a price tag of $5, and he paid the debt off from his paper route funds at a rate of $0.50 a week. Those warm memories of learning to drive in the Model T prompted him to purchase a replica of the car in 1985 for $5,000.

When Furton died in 2006 at the age of eighty-two, he was hailed as a township treasure and someone whose activism and huge heart would be missed. He was survived by one daughter, three grandchildren, eight great-grandchildren and his business partner and companion of forty-five years, Mary Darden.

3

Clinton Township

I t's been two hundred years since Clinton Township was known as the Moravian Settlement and then briefly as Casino. A couple dozen families called the place home, and the heavily wooded area was flush with lumber and gristmills along the Clinton River. By the 1920s, the area was known as the largest producer of roses in the state, and creameries were also abundant. In fact, for a time during the postwar years, Macomb County was known as both the rose and rhubarb capital of the world thanks to prosperous farms in the township. Today, Clinton Township is situated smack in the middle of Macomb County, with three branches of the Clinton River running through it. At just over twenty-eight square miles, Clinton is the tenth-largest township in the state and home to 100,000 people.

WEISS FAMILY

A Rose Is a Rose Is a Rose

Having large orders come into the Mount Clemens/Clinton Township Rose Gardens, owned and operated by the Weiss family starting in 1920, wasn't unusual, but sending roses to the White House in Washington, D.C., three times a week was pretty special. The standing order, placed during Gerald R. Ford's presidency, meant dozens of beautiful roses were displayed during special events in and around the Oval Office. Presidential roses are just one of the many interesting tales in the Weiss family's eighty-year history: they provided 300 million roses, or 25 million dozen roses, to customers around the world.

In 1920, Paul Weiss, a Prussian immigrant, opened the garden. He borrowed his father's $30,000 lifesavings and went into the business with a partner. By 1925, Paul had paid his father back, and for the next seventy-four years, the family were sole owners of the gardens. Paul's son Frederick, born in 1914, grew up around the business, and after graduating from Dartmouth College, he trained as a banker. Then his grandfather summoned him to Mount Clemens to help his father run the Rose Gardens.

A 2005 presentation at the Clinton Macomb Library by Frederick's son Paul Weiss II told the family story quite colorfully. Paul said his father, Fred, was much different than his grandfather and namesake Paul Sr. "He's like an ambassador, a great looking man including standing 6'4" with movie star looks." Fred was complemented by his soon-to-be-wife, Bernice Smith, whom he married in 1942, just before going off to war.

When Paul II was born to the couple in 1943, he became the third generation to grow roses in his family—and all three were born in month of August. The gardens covered just over eight acres with a quarter of million individual rose plants producing four million flowers annually. All watering was done by hand; there was no automation.

Paul Weiss II said that from 1941 to 1946, they made fifty cents on the dollar and never met that rate again. The family had a great lifestyle because of it—at least that's what his father told him, since he was just a small child.

Another huge and unique way the Rose Gardens stood out in that period was an unusual step his father took in 1943. Frederick Weiss petitioned the U.S. government and asked if he could relocate some Japanese American families who were interned in camps during the war. After getting the OK, Frederick Weiss brought twelve families to Clinton Township to live and work in the Rose Gardens. Some moved into apartments built for them on the garden property, while others lived in duplexes in Mount Clemens. Their children went to school, and the community assimilated them into the social structure seamlessly.

A few personal childhood memories Paul Weiss shared include the time in 1947 when the whole east side of the Clinton River Road and Cass Avenue were under two feet of water. Noting that this was the first active memory he had of his grandfather, at just three years old Paul Weiss II recalled he and his dad were in a rowboat inside the greenhouse due to the flooding and they didn't have to water the rose plants on that side of the river for quite a few days. He also remembered the Saturday mornings when his father would

Right: Paul Weiss with his father, Fred Weiss, at the Mount Clemens/ Clinton Township Rose Gardens. *Courtesy of the Weiss family*.

Below: Paul Weiss with a group of Japanese growers and horticulturists at the Mount Clemens/ Clinton Township Rose Gardens. *Courtesy of the Weiss family*.

take him to the greenhouses and his grandfather would say, "If he's here put him to work." Soon a custom set of wading boots in young Paul's size arrived, and he spent the mornings watering two benches of flowers.

After the war, most of the Japanese families went back to California, but one man, George, stayed and worked at the greenhouses for the next forty years. Paul Weiss II said the man taught him about respect, honor and hard work, and he never met anyone with a greater worth ethic. The Weiss family used to stop by George's house on New Year's Day to honor him for what he'd given to the company.

The family patriarch, Paul Weiss, died in 1950 at age sixty from skin cancer, and the business was left to his son and soon to his grandson Paul II. Initially, passing the torch to that third generation wasn't so smooth. Paul Weiss II said while he attended college, he spent summers pulling weeds, removing dirt and replacing fresh dirt in the gardens. He also spent many Saturdays at Eastern Market selling funeral roses and those flowers that hadn't turned out quite right, with his father, Frederick, assuring him the experience would help him build a good character.

After college, Paul II, a finance and economics degree in hand, went to work as a stockbroker. He recalled that, in reality, he always wanted to work in the family business, but his father wrote him a two-page, single-spaced letter about why he shouldn't. Yet Paul II returned to the gardens to work in 1966. He followed the same rules as every other employee and worked sixty hours a week for $1.55 an hour, rotating through all the departments until he learned every aspect of the business. He kept the books for the business, too, and his father gave him $100 a month to do so. The work wasn't glamorous; the temperature would soar to 115 degrees in the greenhouses with 95 percent humidity.

The development of a new flower in the late 1960s, the Forever Rose, proved the salvation for the business, and it became the core product. For a time, it represented 85 percent of the product they grew. In 1969, Paul's father said the gardens needed a new and better power source, as they were utilizing too much coal. He gave Paul II a budget of $200,000 to build and construct the best powerplant he could create. He accomplished the task, cutting expenses but not quality wherever he could. He personally rolled a fuel oil tank the size of a small mobile home off a truck, which saved him $4,000 in crane costs.

When the rose industry in the United States took a big hit from foreign importers in the 1980s, the Weiss Rose Gardens closed in 1999 after eight decades in a business. For many years, the Weiss gardens dominated the

Paul Weiss preparing roses for shipment to the White House during President Gerald Ford's presidency. *Courtesy of the Weiss family.*

industry. At times, Weiss greenhouses produced more than six million roses annually from ten acres along the Clinton River in Clinton Township just outside Mount Clemens. Today, the property houses a subdivision called Rose Garden Estates.

Paul Weiss II said that "a business is the sum of the people who make it happen," and that's what he missed most once the family business closed. Paul Weiss II died at age sixty-three in December 2006, a businessman with an activist's heart.

DONALD GREEN

An Affable Historian and Tireless Volunteer

The first time Clinton Township Historical Society president James Hungerford met Donald Green, the gregarious fellow "was up to his eyebrows in the tall vegetation, hot, sweaty and very happy." Sounds about right in describing Green, a longtime community activist and historian, who encountered Hungerford while clearing a trail in the newly acquired township property along the Clinton River that later became Canal Park. Clearing the way for new things became Green's path in life.

Green was born in December 1925 in Mount Clemens, Michigan, to Stuart and Marjorie Green. A veteran of World War II, he served in the U.S. Air Force, returned home, got a business degree from Wayne State University and then went to work in his family's very successful business, M.L. Green and Son Jewelers. He represented the third generation in the Green family to become local jewelers, behind his grandfather and his father, Stuart. He soon watched his own children follow in those footsteps to embrace the family legacy. He married Ludomira H. Zaremba in 1949, and they raised three boys in Clinton Township.

Despite great business success, Green's heart belonged to his community, and he spent decades volunteering on projects to benefit others. He was a longtime member of the Mount Clemens Rotary Club, served on the Mount Clemens General Hospital Board of Trustees (now known as McLaren Macomb) for over fifty years and was a member of the North Star Sail Club.

He parlayed his love of history back into the community, too, serving on the Macomb County Historical Commission and as president of the Clinton Township Historical Society. Green recruited Hungerford to the Historic Commission, and they worked together to research the 1782 Moravian Settlement along the Clinton River, Their collaboration led to Woody Park, the establishment of the Don Green Trail connecting Canal Park with Budd Park and the creation of the Clinton and Kalamazoo Historical Societies.

The other area where Green truly left his mark was in the establishment of the Clinton-Macomb Township Library. Library Director Larry Neal said Green was a mentor and friend for twenty years, and his energy and ability to engage others made the library, which opened in 2003, possible. As president of the Library Board, Green was actually Neal's boss, and one of the most important things he taught the new director was "no surprises"—don't ever let the board hear something is going on after the fact, keep an open line of communication.

The library, often referred to as Green's crown jewel, had him as a board member for a dozen years, ten as the president. His hard work made him the recipient of the American Library Association's Trustee of the Year award in 2008. Today, the library services 180,000 patrons and handles one million transactions a year.

Four-generation portrait of the family of Merritt L. Green, who established his jewelry business in Mount Clemens in 1907. *From left to right*: Merritt L. Green, his son Stuart A. Green and grandson Donald W. Green. Shown in the center is great-grandson Gregory Green. *From the* Macomb Daily.

None of this surprised Hungerford, who said Green was definitely a guy who got things done and had a salesman's way of convincing people that donating property or money or time was actually in their own best interest. Good friends for several decades, Hungerford said Green loved classical

Donald Green, 2008. *Courtesy of Michael Robinson.*

music, good food and fine wine. His favorite sporting pastimes were tennis and sailing, and he loved nature and was very concerned about climate change.

In 2009, Green worked on the Tomlinson Arboretum in Clinton Township, part of which is a designated path called the Don Green Way, where more than one thousand trees have been planted on a twenty-four-acre parcel.

Several highlights in Green's personal life included when he became an Eagle Scout and his grandson followed suit, the time he was named the grand marshal for the Clinton Township Gratiot Cruise and the world traveling he was blessed to enjoy with his wife of nearly seventy years.

When Green passed away in August 2019 at the age of ninety-three, all who knew him realized he was a man who was not only irreplaceable but would also be warmly remembered in the community for years to come.

4

Macomb Township

ounded in 1834, the township was named to honor General Alexander Macomb, a distinguished veteran of the War of 1812. One of the first major farming communities, consisting of mostly dairy farms, Macomb's wooded areas were also plentiful, prompting the opening of several sawmills. By 1845, the township had a strong presence of German immigrants who were expert farmers and made their homes in an area within the township known as Waldenburg. Romeo Plank Road was an extremely important thoroughfare in the early development of the township. It was actually called "Plank Road" for many years because it used to be made of nothing but wooden planks. This road was significant because it was the main route farmers took and so many people traveled along this path it was turned into a toll road. For many years, the road was simply made out of wood, and it was only paved in the last fifty years. Today, the township has grown beyond simple farmland and includes numerous residences and businesses over 36.3 square miles with a population of 88,000.

STIER FAMILY

Waldenburg's Hometown Hardware

When German immigrant George Stier arrived in Macomb Township in 1857, he brought his farming expertise to a small hamlet within the township known to locals as Waldenburg. He purchased forty acres near 22 Mile and Romeo Plank Road, joining a large population of mostly immigrant German farmers. In the nineteenth century, Waldenburg was a stop along the plank toll road that connected Romeo, Michigan, to Mount Clemens and Romeo Plank Road had stations every few miles along the way to collect tolls or give the horses a rest.

In 1903, George's son Louis opened Stier's Hardware in a section nearby that had become the business center for Waldenburg. In time, the store was turned over to Louis's son William, who, like his father, was active in the community, serving as the township constable and on several township boards.

By 1950, the third generation of Stier men had taken over the hardware store. Carl Stier, William's son, became the proprietor and also stepped up to help the township form its first Lion Club and a volunteer fire department. Shelley Stier Henshaw, seventy-five, picks up the story from here, sharing memories clear back to when she was just five years old and her family moved into an eight-hundred-square-foot apartment attached to the hardware store so her father, Carl, could run the place. The family included her parents and three siblings, so space was at a premium, but she has wonderful memories just the same.

Shelley Henshaw's grandfather William originally sold old car parts in the store, but once her father, Carl, took over, the stock evolved to include farm equipment and farming tools plus a huge variety of other items, similar to a general store. Everything from cattle prods to carpet sweepers crowded the shelves, and Henshaw said her father began to display hardware memorabilia around the store too. The experience became quite an adventure for the whole family simply because if you lived in the store you worked in the store. Henshaw loved helping the customers. She soon grew proficient in reaching her hand into a bin of nails, grabbing a handful and placing them on a scale that quickly revealed she had magically pulled out exactly one pound, as requested by the patron.

Toys, including cap guns, whistles, kazoos and rubber balls, for the nominal price of ten to fifteen cents, filled the shelves, and many customers put the items on layaway for their kids for Christmas. As hurried parents started showing up on Christmas Eve to pick up their purchases, the air filled with excitement for the holiday. Henshaw recalled how many of the farmers would step back into the hardware's storage area to have some holiday cheer with her dad.

Children—including Henshaw and her siblings, Dennis, Jeffrey and Carole—who lived on the farms in the tight-knit community attended

The Stier family in front of their hardware store in Waldenburg, a burg in Macomb Township. *Courtesy of Shelley Stier Henshaw.*

The Stier family at the turn of the twentieth century. *Courtesy of Shelly Stier Henshaw.*

school in Mount Clemens but were simply referred to as "Waldenburg kids." They enjoyed a carefree adventurous childhood swimming, skating and exploring the little burg they called home. Henshaw holds particularly fond memories of visiting the store while her grandfather owned it and, later, while living there, rummaging through the attic, which was packed because previous generations threw nothing away. An old wooden coffin, logs with bark still attached to them and literally hundreds of other trinkets were discovered—although most ended up at the local dump. Shelley Henshaw recalled the old store:

> *The Stier Hardware was always the center of the neighborhood, where people of all ages could simply drop in to have their skates sharpened on the way to the ice pond, get a fish taken off a line or buy food for their pet turtle. The shop was a familiar gathering place for members of the community because they all knew they could count on the Stiers to open even if it was late at night or on a Sunday. Customers would just sit down at the family's Sunday dinner table and wait for Carl Stier to finish his meal and then open the store.*

In 1979, the Stier Hardware Store was passed on to the fourth generation when Jeffrey Stier took over the business. He incorporated repair work for lawnmowers and other equipment, but a rough economy and the advent of big-box stores carrying everything from groceries to hardware prompted the closing of the shop in 2008. The building remained empty and abandoned before it was demolished in 2013, a 110-year-old landmark lost to the past.

Despite time and progress in the township, the Waldenburg name remains in two original buildings still standing and open for business: the Waldenburg Bar, next door to where the Stier Hardware once was, and across the street, a corner market that used to be a tavern with a popular dance hall on its second floor. In fact, Henshaw, who was crushed to see her family's legacy torn down, remains thankful for her memories: like falling asleep as a small child while listening to the sounds of the music from the dance hall every Saturday night and as a young mother pushing her baby stroller along with a friend to stop in the tavern and have a beer on a hot summer day. She's now become the family historian, gathering photos and memorabilia from her past, and she recently donated original Waldenburg/Macomb Township polling boxes, dating to 1908, to the Macomb Township Historical Commission.

AMBROSE LEYER

The Cobbler of Waldenburg

When Ambrose Leyer was born in March 1840 near Austrian Silesia, which is now Czechoslovakia, his family could barely feed the mouths they already had, so he was turned over to an uncle, August Posner, to be raised in a nearby town. In time, young Ambrose had to become an apprentice and learn a trade, so he picked the profession of cobbler. Too small to be drafted into the military, Leyer became very proficient in his craft and was eventually sent to a soldiers' camp outside his town to make sure they were taken care of properly with new shoes. Several years passed, and Uncle Posner packed up his belongings and moved to America, settling in Waldenburg, where he established a brickyard.

Ambrose was nearly twenty when letters from his Uncle August arrived in Silesia stating that the Lutheran Church he had joined in Waldenburg had no musical instruments. As luck would have it, the uncle's old congregation in Europe had recently replaced all of its old instruments and offered them to Uncle August for free but asked that he pay thirty-five dollars for one additional instrument that was so special it played anything one's heart might desire. The fee was quickly gathered in donations from members of the Waldenburg congregation, and the shipment was soon on its way to the United States.

The congregation and Uncle August were delighted some six weeks later to discover that the special instrument was in fact his nephew Ambrose Leyer. He had traveled across the ocean aboard a sailing vessel with boxes of used musical instruments, including trombones, his passage covered by the church's thirty-five-dollar donation. Not long after his arrival in town, Leyer bought ten acres of land in Waldenburg, setting up his home and cobbler shop inside an abandoned toll gate off Romeo Plane Road. Sometimes Lever enjoyed filling his leisure hours by traveling to nearby Mount Clemens, where a training camp was set up in a wooded area near the Clinton River. Watching the soldiers, many of them only able to speak German, struggle to understand their officers' orders was amusing to Lever. He said German soldiers he encountered in camps back home were drilled with strict precision, but here they couldn't sort out the language enough to follow any orders. Finally, a young German boy selling cigars in the camp was recruited to explain the drills to the soldiers, as he spoke English as well as his native language.

Members of the Ambrose Leyer family at their homestead and farm in Waldenburg. *Courtesy of Shelley Stier Henshaw.*

In time, the "cobbler of Waldenburg" married Christiane Johana Kluge, and they had nine children; several didn't make it past infancy, but five survived their parents. Leyer's wife, Christiane, died at the age of fifty-five; it was reported that she fell face-down into a feather bed and smothered before the predicament was discovered. In contrast, the cobbler lived to celebrate ninety-three birthdays. One daughter lived with him on the Waldenburg farm, taking care of his meals and home, while a son tended the ten acres. He said the secret to his longevity was plenty of plain food, regular hours, steady work and beer in moderation. Having lived through the era of Prohibition, he also proclaimed that it was the worst fate any nation could endure because it made people drink more products that weren't at all good for them. In fact, he said the beers brought to him during Prohibition were nowhere near as good as the ones he enjoyed at home in Germany or in Waldenburg, compliments of the village brewer, who produced his own beer in the general store.

KUCHENMEISTER FAMILY

Generations of Business Sense

It's rare to trace a family back over two hundred years and discover so many business-minded men that all found success in different fields. For the Kuchenmeister clan, it started with Frederick Kuchenmeister, who emigrated from Germany in 1860 and moved to Waldenburg in Macomb Township. By 1863, he had purchased land and became a carpenter and a farmer. In time, the Kuchenmeister farm was one of the largest and most well known in the area, with lots of sales made through the farm. One of those early enterprises was a dairy farm; they made butter from all the milk, and Frederick traveled to Detroit in a buckboard wagon to sell the fresh butter. Legend has it that when he decided to build a brick house, he took the butter to the city and traded it for bricks. It took two years to get enough bricks to build a home. Frederick Kuchenmeister lived at the farm until his death in 1914, and his homestead is now registered as a historical site in Macomb Township.

Sophia and Frederick Kuchenmeiser, whose family emigrated from Germany in 1860. *Courtesy of the Kuchenmeister family.*

Over the next several decades, Frederick's son Albert Kuchenmeister ran the family farm for a time and then moved to a farm in nearby New Haven, where his four children were born. Albert was an enterprising fellow and was forever starting new businesses while moving his family all over town. The list included stores, gas stations and real estate across metro Detroit—and, at one point, a citrus farm in Texas. Returning to Michigan, Albert next tried his hand in the reclaimed oil business; this venture was short lived, and he next rented land and ran a gas station near 23 Mile and Gratiot Avenue. Over the years, his four sons—Carl, Walter, Louis and Frederick—worked alongside their father or at times at local car companies and the New Haven Foundry.

Frederick Kuchenmeister, whose grandfather had come to Macomb Township in 1860, was also a go-getter. In the 1930s, he was an auto parts wholesaler basically working from a panel van. He would drive south down Gratiot Avenue toward Detroit, stopping at various auto parts manufacturers. The business gene was passed on to Frederick's son, Wayne Frederick Kuchenmeister, who was born in 1935.

Wayne grew up in Roseville near 14-Mile Road and Gratiot. During World War II, he was too young to be a soldier and his father too old, so Fredrick just continued his business with limited supplies due to rationing. In high school, Wayne's height topped out at five feet, eight inches, a full five inches shorter that his father. He wasn't very athletic, but he did finish the Boy Scouts of America challenges, ultimately earning his Eagle Scout status. On his graduation day, Wayne purchased and drove his dream car, a 1947 Chrysler Town and Country convertible. He would forever be a convertible fan and owned at least one at all times. In the early 1970s, he actually purchased a 1947 model and restored it to its original condition.

In 1954, Wayne married Barbara Faye Belcher, and they had three children: Cheryl, Rock and Russell. Always eager to learn new things, Wayne worked at a gas station and a tubing company and then was hired as a warehouse manager for the Andrew Young Company, an electrical parts sales agency. He soon moved to outside sales, and for the next two years, Wayne traveled Michigan, selling to the electrical industry. Faye and the children often spent the day driving around Michigan with him, packing lunches and eating in public parks. Meanwhile, Wayne's father tried unsuccessfully to persuade him to join the auto parts business. However, Wayne now had the electrical wholesale business in his sights. When Mill & Howard Wholesale closed its business in Mount Clemens, he

Norman and Wayne Kuchenmeister opened Kuchenmeister Electric Supply. *Courtesy of the Kuchenmeister family.*

recognized the potential of the local electrical market and began to search for a building to start his own business.

For the new business, he wanted a working partner, so he and his brother Norman opened Kuchenmeister Electric Supply inside an old feed shed in Mount Clemens. Their seed money came from their father, Frederick. The first business slogan was simply "Service," but it later became "Who serves you faster? Kuchenmeister." Offering fast service along with hard work and family cooperation created a very successful electrical wholesale business for more than twenty-five years.

Throughout their years as owners of a successful local business, the Kuchenmeister brothers shared their good fortune with the community, donating to many worthy causes. In 1987, they even presented the city of Mount Clemens with a check for $20,000 to fund the construction of a gazebo downtown that remains in place today.

In 1987, after a quarter of a century together, the brothers decided it was time to divide the business up for the next generation. Wayne's division became the K/E Electric Supply Corporation, which was turned over to his children. Though he often told people he was going to retire, Wayne could be found wearing various hats from counter salesman to warehouse manager, public relations director, storyteller and specific problem solver— although his favorite title was coordinator.

Wayne passed away in 2010 at the age of seventy-five, and his wife, Barbara Faye, followed him to heaven in 2015. Today, the family business remains strong with four locations and the children at the helm. Many of the quiet contributions and donations made to the community over the years by their parents continues today through the Sandbox Foundation. It was established in 2015 by Rock and Cheryl Kuchenmeister and allows them to utilize their inheritance to fund scholarships for local college students.

5

Memphis

*T*he entire city of Memphis is just one square mile but actually falls in both Macomb and St. Clair Counties. Settled in 1835, by the Wells family, the property was known as the Wells Settlement until 1848, when it was renamed Memphis in honor of the ancient city along the Nile in Egypt. Memphis, Michigan, was incorporated as a city in 1865. Today, the city remains a testament to small-town America with just 1,200 residents, small businesses on Main Street, football at the high school on Friday nights and an annual summer festival dubbed Duck Days with a rubber ducky race along the Belle River concluding the festivities.

HARLAN PERRY HOWARD

Farm Boy to Country Music Songwriter

For someone who grew up during the Depression while being shuffled between orphanages and foster homes, landing on your feet as a successful songwriter in Nashville sounded like a fairy tale. Yet it's the tale Harlan Perry Howard lived as he went from farm chores in rural northern Macomb County to sitting alongside country greats like Patsy Cline, Conway Twitty and Buck Owens.

Howard, who was seventy-four when he passed away in 2002 following a heart attack, left behind a catalogue of four thousand songs, including

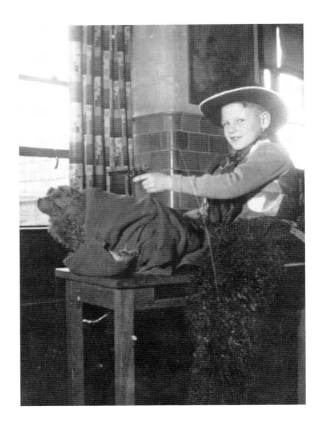

A young Harlan Howard in a photo that was published in the local newspapers so his mother would come and claim him at the state foster home. *Courtesy of Melanie Smith-Howard.*

hundreds of tunes that topped the country and pop music charts spanning five decades.

It's an impressive legacy that's being kept alive by his wife, Melanie Smith-Howard, via a publishing company and a website packed with memories and mementos devoted to her late husband. Howard was born in Detroit in 1927 to Evelyn Steed Howard and Ralph Howard, both natives of Ohio who moved to Michigan to work in the auto industry. He was the third son, with two older brothers named Wallace and Milton.

As Smith-Howard tells it, Evelyn Howard left her husband after Harlan's birth and initially took him with her but soon returned him to his father, Ralph. A heavy drinker, he was declared unfit, and Harlan, four, was placed in an orphanage. He stayed there until he was eight. Evelyn was located, and the state demanded she go pick up her son. Harlan's brother Wallace died of a head injury at thirteen, and Milton was put into a home for wayward boys. Reunited with his mother, Harlan was a hoodlum by age eight, and living with his mother and her boyfriend wasn't working out. He constantly taunted his half-brother, who was albino and legally blind, and the parents had enough of it, Smith-Howard said.

Evelyn was pregnant and feared another failed relationship if Harlan stayed, so she found a family on the outskirts of town to take him in. Harlan stayed with the Grant family for three years and was removed by the state and placed with another family and then another and another. Harlan lived in numerous foster homes. He spent time in Memphis and Leslie, Michigan.

In an interview in *American Songwriter Magazine* (September/October 1990), "A Tribute to Harlan Howard," the songwriter recalled as a boy he started listening to Ernest Tubbs on the radio and tried to memorize the lyrics to all his songs. As a twelve-year-old foster kid working on a farm, Harlan said he was impressed by both "the tragedy and the heart and soul" Tubbs put into his songs.

Scrambling to recall and write down the words to Tubbs tunes, Howard couldn't always get the latter verses, so he began making up his own words for the lyrics.

"The logical evolution was to write a whole song from scratch, so I did that, I was this farm kid bored with chores and school and I had all the time in the world," Howard quipped. He also hated the name *Harlan* and went by the name Tom Howard during his youth.

He joined the army at eighteen and was sent to Fort Benning, Georgia, to train as a paratrooper. He thought he was going to see the world, but they made him a jump master at Fort Benning. He had learned to play a few chords on the guitar, and the guys kept him there so he could entertain them, Smith-Howard said.

After his service in the army was over, Harlan went back to Michigan to find his mother. She had a few more kids by then. Her husband, Joe, had a jukebox operation, and he hired Harlan to help him with his route.

After a few years in Michigan, Harlan moved to California to be closer to a music scene. Toiling in a factory by day, Harlan spent evenings in his boardinghouse bedroom writing songs. After introducing himself to several local country music stars who recorded several of his songs, royalty checks began to arrive. Harlan packed his bags and moved to Nashville.

Harlan was married to singer and Grand Old Opera Star Jan Howard for a dozen years; her son, his stepson, James Van Howard, was killed in action during the Vietnam War.

After establishing himself as a successful songwriter in Nashville, Harlan counted "I Fall to Pieces" by Patsy Cline, "Why Not Me" by The Judds and

A publicity photo for country music star Harlan Howard. *Courtesy of Jim McGuire.*

"She's Gone, Gone, Gone," recorded by Glen Campbell among the dozens of hits he penned over the years. Harlan had as many as fifteen songs on the Country Top 40 at one time—an amazing feat that has yet to be equaled, Smith-Howard said.

He was inducted into the Nashville Songwriters Hall of Fame in 1973 and, in 1997, both the Country Music Hall of Fame and the Songwriters Hall of Fame. Although he has influenced several generations of songwriters, his greatest sense of accomplishment came from helping "juvenile" songwriters along the way.

A Harlan cowriter commented,

> *Harlan looked at songwriting differently than other writers—it was the love of his life. I think what he contributed to the songwriting community is that he made writers feel it's important to be a songwriter. It's a career; it's not just something you do for a while and go on to something else. Harlan was 100 percent songwriter all the time.*

EVA MCCALL HAMILTON

Green Onions, STDs and the Michigan Senate

A champion for both women and children's rights, Eva McCall Hamilton certainly left her mark as the first woman in the United States elected to serve in the state legislature in 1920.

She was born on December 13, 1871, in St. Clair County, the second child of John A. and Anna (Petree) McCall, who were of Irish, English and Scottish descent and owned a farm in Memphis. She had four siblings, an older brother, Pearce, and three younger brothers, Arthur, Frank and John, according to an 1880 census record.

After graduating from Memphis High School, Hamilton moved to Grand Rapids to become a teacher. She also met and married her husband, Charles Hamilton, who was the proprietor of a large furniture market in the city. Valerie Marvin, historian and curator for the Michigan State Capitol, said Hamilton was actually a physical education instructor, which was an up-and-coming profession for women at the time, as there was a real sense that women needed to be more physically active.

She was also involved with many organizations locally and statewide that worked to promote the suffrage movement. In 1910, that included participating in a parade for the cause that had a large float and fifty cars decorated with signs in favor of giving women the right to vote. Hamilton held the reins of the horse leading the "Lilly Float for Suffragists" in Grand Rapids' annual downtown homecoming parade.

Marvin said in 1912, a bid to pass a suffrage referendum was introduced in Michigan and was defeated by only a narrow margin after an intense fight, and Hamilton played a significant role, albeit on the losing side that time out.

Then Michigan governor Chase Osborn commended her efforts toward the suffrage movement in a letter dated March 1912 when he wrote, "I think no one has done better work for the cause than you."

She was also known to travel to the state capitol in Lansing to speak before lawmakers on any number of topics prior to being elected herself in 1920.

Closer to her home in Grand Rapids, the future senator remained active in community and civic affairs and was instrumental in seeing farmers' markets approved and established downtown.

As the story goes, Hamilton used to carry baskets of fresh vegetables around town to promote her market idea and soon became known as the "Green Onion Lady" because her handouts included plenty of scallions.

Given her civic-minded agenda, no one was surprised to see her put her name on the ballot to fill a state senate seat as a Republican representing the Sixteenth District from Grand Rapids in 1920. Her timing was quite fortuitous. The Nineteenth Amendment to the Constitution giving women the right to vote had finally passed in 1919, and Hamilton was elected, winning 14,294 votes versus 7,536 for her Democratic opponent, according to a story in the November 3, 1920 *Lansing State Journal*.

Hamilton, then forty-nine, was sworn into office in 1921, the only female senator in the United States. She had an uncle in the state senate at the time, Thomas McCall, who helped her network, but she had no plan to profit from his name, continuing to call herself Eva M. Hamilton.

After being sworn in, Hamilton was celebrated with much fanfare, including attention from the national media, and was welcomed to the senate floor, where her desk was covered with flowers.

Despite the historic victory, Marvin said the overall feeling by her male colleagues was that women did not belong in government, period. Practical

Eva McCall Hamilton at the signing of a bill at the statehouse in Lansing. *Courtesy of the Library of Michigan, an agency of the Michigan Department of Education.*

jokes weren't out of the question either, and in one incident, some colleagues filled her briefcase with bricks to see if she could pick it up.

Under such scrutiny, Hamilton felt she not only represented Grand Rapids but also half of the state of Michigan, specifically the female half, all looking to her to see if she would pick sides or fall under the spell of her male counterparts, Marvin said.

They didn't need to worry.

If having a woman seated in the senate chamber wasn't shocking enough, one of the first bills Hamilton threw her support behind was one that would require men and women seeking marriage licenses to first be tested for social diseases.

Marvin noted that the subject of STDs was actually quite a hot topic across the nation at the time; after World War I, there was a huge influx of disease nationwide. "This was the first bill she spoke about on the floor, and personally, I think it was a very brave thing for her to do," Marvin added. "And when she was done with speaking, even the men who opposed the bill congratulated her for her bravery."

A story in the *Detroit Free Press* at the time read:

> *Mrs. Hamilton, in a voice that was low although it reached the corner most areas of the gallery where a number of women legislators were seated, said, "but we legislate cleanliness if the passage of this bill will prevent innocent girls from contracting marriage with men with communicable diseases. I feel that it will have accomplished a great deal."*

Despite Hamilton's memorable speech on the matter, the bill failed, but she was not deterred, introducing a dozen more during her two-year tenure and seeing at least six of them passed on the senate floor. Marvin said Hamilton was instrumental in getting the Mother's Pension Reform Bill passed, which would ensure funding for underprivileged children and allow them to remain at home instead of being turned over to state institutions, including poor farms and reform schools.

Marvin said in the early nineteenth century, a child was often considered an orphan if the father died, and the mother actually didn't automatically garner custody of her own child. As many widows struggled to provide for their children, some were forced to give them up so they didn't starve. The new pension bill provided a subsidiary to single mothers to help feed their children and keep them at home.

Official portrait of Eva McCall Hamilton, by Larry Blovits. *Michigan State Capitol Archives.*

Hamilton didn't win reelection in 1923, but she certainly left her mark and continued to do so as she returned to Grand Rapids and private life.

She was a big part of launching what is now known as the League of Women Voters in our state. "She was a lifelong reformer who just sort of forged on ahead; she certainly wasn't just a blip and she's gone," Marvin said.

When Hamilton returned to the state capitol in 1946 to be formally honored with a resolution recognizing her contribution to the senate, she was disappointed to find that no other women had followed in her footsteps to Lansing.

Hamilton died of heart failure in 1948 at the age of seventy-five, just two weeks after her husband passed away. In another nod to her pioneering nature, Hamilton asked to be cremated, which was an unusual request for the time. It is rumored that per her request, her ashes were spread over her father's grave.

In the 1990s, Michigan legislatures passed a resolution to honor significant lawmakers from the past by hanging portraits of each one in the senate chamber. Hamilton is among them. In fact, Hamilton's portrait attracts a lot of attention among the fifty portraits around the building, a large majority of them male governors.

Hamilton was inducted into the Michigan Women's Hall of Fame in 2012.

SHIRLEY ARDELL MASON

Shy Art Teacher Was Sybil

Shirley Ardell Mason spent several years as a quiet but likable art teacher with Memphis Community Schools in the early 1950s, but nobody knew that her dark and troubled childhood would soon make her a household name.

Mason was born in 1923 in Dodge Center, Minnesota, the only child of Walter Wingfield Mason (a carpenter and architect) and Martha Alice Atkinson. After graduating from college with a teaching degree, it wasn't until nearly middle age that Mason underwent psychoanalysis under psychiatrist Cornelia Wilbur and her multiple personality traits were unveiled. The condition was said to be prompted by extreme abuse on the part of Mason's mother when she was a child.

In 1973, Flora Rheta Schrieber's nonfiction book *Sybil: The True Story of a Woman Possessed by 16 Separate Personalities* sold millions of copies and outlined Mason's treatment for dissociative identity disorder, also referred to as multiple personality disorder. The book was made into an award-winning TV movie in 1976 starring Sally Field and Joanne Woodward, and a remake in 2007 featured actresses Tammy Blanchard and Jessica Lange.

The timid art instructor pictured in the 1952 Memphis High School yearbook had become infamous, and her case was researched by Memphis Historical Society member Ruth Koppinger Suwalkowski. People were skeptical about Suwalkowski's discovery, so she pursued the story, learning Mason moved north of Detroit to Memphis to teach school in the early 1950s. Suwalkowski also found an article in the local newspaper from that period that featured Mason with several of her paintings. Today, that painting appears when any Google search is conducted related to Sybil or Mason.

Once word got out that Mason and Sybil were the same person, many of her former students reacted with surprise and shock. They remembered her as quiet, reserved and sweet but endlessly supportive of those interested in art. One student said she had no idea her art teacher had different personalities, and she found her to be a very kind, caring and loving person. In fact, Mason's tutoring led this student to develop a love of art.

Mason had a habit of gifting artwork to fellow teachers at Memphis High School and sometimes to students as well. There are several newspapers stories from the early 1950s noting her work with students at art shows, and her own work was featured in an America Artists Series in St. Louis in 1954.

Above: Shirley Mason with one of her paintings. *Google Docs.*

Right: Memphis High School art director Shirley Mason in 1953. *Memphis Historical Society.*

ART DIRECTOR

Row 1: Mrs. Pearsall, Miss Mason, Mrs. Will, Mrs. Raymond, Mrs. Jeska, Mrs. Doty,
Row 2: Miss Braidwood, Mrs. Shobbrook, Miss Bartlett, Mrs. Likins, Mrs. Wisuri.
Row 3: Mr. Beedle, Mr. Talley, Mr. Backas, Mr. Kring, Mr. Dolan, Mr. Brauer.

Faculty photo from the 1953 Memphis High School yearbook with Shirley Mason. *Memphis Historical Society.*

The article states that Mason taught at Memphis Community Schools and that her paintings had appeared in galleries across fourteen states.

Mason resigned her teaching position in Memphis at the conclusion of the 1954 school year and moved to New York to continue to pursue her career in art studies at Columbia University.

One particular painting that Mason gifted to a Memphis student in the 1950s definitely reflects her style, according to author Nancy Preston. A longtime personal friend of Mason's, Preston wrote the book *After Sybil... From the Letters of Shirley Mason*, the story of her life after the integration of her sixteen personalities. Preston met Mason in 1970 when she registered for an art class at Rio Grande College in Rio Grande Ohio where Mason was an associate professor.

Describing that first encounter with Mason in class that fall, Preston said she found an unassuming, rather plain middle-aged woman but someone committed to encouraging even the most novice artist. When a fellow student stated that the he couldn't really draw at all, Preston recalls Mason's upbeat reply, "Well, I'm here to help you, not to be an art critic, so don't be afraid to try." The simple exchange allowed many of her students who were worried about their artistic abilities, including Preston, to relax in the knowledge that Mason was on their side.

After forging a friendship beyond the classroom, Mason eventually revealed her secret identity to Preston, which solidified their twenty-eight-year association that included letters, phone calls and personal visits.

Looking at the piece of art Mason gifted to the Memphis High School student, Preston said it was both interesting and revealing. The tree branches resemble hands or claws that are reaching upward while the focal point seems to be an enclosed area in the middle of the painting. The style is evident in many of Mason's pieces and indicative of her desire to escape her mother's hands and that she felt trapped. Preston added that she has two of Mason's original paintings from after completion of her therapy, and there is a vast difference between her art pre-therapy with Dr. Wilbur and post-therapy after the integration of her personalities.

Having been a student in Mason's classroom, Preston said what she admired about her was that she was interested in everyone and focused on their success as they worked to create their own art, regardless of the quality of the masterpieces. Teaching was important to her because as a talented artist herself, she was sharing a piece of herself in a good way and because of her Dissociative Identity Disorder (DID), prior to therapy, teaching was an outlet for some of her alters to connect with the outside world. Preston said she also admired Mason for her bravery in overcoming DID and living a good life.

Mason, who retired in Lexington, Kentucky, died in 1998 at the age of seventy-five following a breast cancer battle. A stash that included 103 paintings found locked in the basement of Mason's home following an estate sale was dubbed the "Hidden Paintings," and many were unsigned and thought to have been created by one of her alternate personalities.

JOHN AND THOMAS CLEGG

The "Real" First Auto aka The Thing

Michigan's first self-propelled vehicle on record was built in Memphis in the winter of 1884 by John and Thomas Clegg. The father-and-son mechanics built the vehicle even before Henry Ford's experiments with automobile travel began. The four-seated "car" ran under the power of a single-cylinder steam engine with a tubular boiler in the rear. Leather belts transferred the power to the 5'8" rear wheels, and soft coal was used for fuel. The duo casually called their creation "the contraption" and later just settled on naming it "The Thing."

Also often referred to at times as "The Cleggmobile," the vehicle has an interesting history, with its first run taking place in the spring of 1885, a ride to Emmett, Michigan. The round trip was fourteen miles. Thomas Clegg made thirty test runs totaling five hundred miles and was the first to drive a self-propelled car in Michigan and possibly the nation. The car was dismantled two years later. The engine was sold to George M. Granger of Port Huron to use in his creamery.

Thomas Clegg said that following the death of his father in 1888, he didn't have the money or the time to continue to experiment. Years later, Henry Ford offered to buy the machine shop for placement at Greenfield Village, but the offer came too late: Thomas Clegg had already torn the building down in 1936.

Thomas Clegg died in May 1939. The Cleggs' work is still considered the first automobile in the country. A historic marker has been placed near the machine shop where the father and son built the vehicle, at Bordman Road and Cedar Street in Memphis. Despite its notoriety, there were no photographs of the unique vehicle, and any references to the car were destroyed in a house fire at Thomas Clegg's home in 1929.

Memphis City councilman and historical society member Larry Wilson shows off a model of "The Thing" that he donated to the city's historical society. *From the* Macomb Daily.

Those facts weren't going to stop longtime car enthusiast and current Memphis city councilman Larry Wilson and his wife, Evelyn. The couple, longtime Memphis residents and history buffs, commissioned Richard Hess of nearby Emmett, Michigan, to build a replica of "The Thing" so they could donate it to the Memphis Historical Society in 2018.

Larry Wilson, eighty-nine, said Hess was going to use his artistic talents to replicate the vehicle, taking Wilson's own research into account, and it would likely be a pretty accurate design. He added that the Cleggs designed one other car in 1886; it was made of brass and weighed 2,800 pounds, but money problems forced the father and son to abandon that project early on.

Should a real sketch or photograph of "The Thing" turn up somewhere now, Larry Wilson said it will be interesting to see how close his research and Hess's talents came to replicating the original model.

6

Mount Clemens

*T*he city first known as High Banks and Big Springs was founded in 1818 by Christian Clemens, who had come to the area a decade earlier and bought property along the river, where he built a log cabin. By 1818, Clemens had platted property for homes and a village that he named Mount Clemens. Three months later, Governor Lewis Cass named Mount Clemens the county seat and appointed Clemens judge of the county court. In 1837, the town was incorporated as a village, and by 1879, the population had grown to over three thousand people. Citizens voted for the village, which covered just 4.2 miles, to become a city. As to industry, an attempt to develop salt wells in the city proved unsuccessful but resulted in the discovery of famed mineral baths that flourished and made Mount Clemens famous throughout the world as a health spa. One reason for the success was that the waters were packed with thirty-four different minerals, and bathers soon claimed that everything from skin eczema to neuralgia was cured. Today, the city is still prosperous and has over sixteen thousand residents.

THE FLYING NELSONS

High Wire Was All in the Family

Most people from large families often feel they are part of a circus, but four generations of the Nelson family, whose home base was Mount Clemens,

Portrait of the Arthur and Sara Nelson family of Mount Clemens, a troupe of professional circus acrobats who made their off-season home in Mount Clemens. *Mount Clemens Library Collection.*

actually performed under the big top for decades. The family business began in London, England, when Robert Nelson Sr., whose surname was actually Hobson, founded an acrobatic troupe with his three brothers. They sailed to the United States in 1886 and toured the states, Cuba and India before they went their separate ways.

Not deterred, Robert Nelson and his two young sons, Robert Jr. and Arthur, formed the Great Nelson Family; they performed as a Risley Act, which has one member of the group lying on his back against a support while balancing and rolling the others while they are performing acrobatic stunts. The new group soon met with great reviews and toured Europe and India, performing with the Dan Rice Circus and P.T. Barnum's Circus.

In 1887, Robert Nelson Sr. adopted Mount Clemens as his family's permanent home, and their house on South Avenue had a specially equipped basement that served as an acrobatic training center for members of his family. Nelson also purchased an old theater on Cass Avenue and operated it as the Nelson Opera House. In late 1896, Arthur Nelson married Sarah Warren, and after forming a tightwire act, they joined the Nelson Family acrobats. The couple soon had six daughters and a son: Rosina, Oneida, Theol, Estrella, Hilda, Carmencita and Paul, who were all trained in the family business from a young age. All of the children but Rosina were born in Mount Clemens.

In 1910, the family, now known as the Flying Nelsons, were performing with the Royal and Adams indoor circus in Buffalo, New York, when a reporter approached Sarah Nelson about life under the big top with her children. At that time, the Nelson family included seven children aged two to eighteen. Sarah Nelson was asked if she though the circus life was in any way detrimental to her children. She quickly replied, "No indeed I do not, do my babies looked harmed?" She also stated that all of her children had been brought up in the carpet bag, a satchel that is taken onstage—the youngest member of the family emerges to do their part in the act. There is said to be an unwritten rule in the circus world that once children can stand on their hands, they are ready to join the act. Of course, the parents weren't asking more of the kids then they'd do themselves. Sarah Nelson was an accomplished acrobat who rode a bicycle on a high wire while her husband, Arthur, was considered the best acrobat in the business.

A publicity photo for the Nelson Family Circus. *Library of Congress.*

Each year, when the circus took a break, the Nelsons returned home to Mount Clemens, and the children even attended school in the local district. Robert Sr., Robert Jr. and a younger brother, Artie, all passed away by 1916, and Arthur then became the head of the family. The family of nine continued to perform under the big top for major circuses, including the John Robinson Circus and Ringling Brothers–Barnum & Bailey, picking up endless accolades along the way. Barnum & Bailey even created a series of lithographs featuring the Nelson sisters Oneida, Rosina, Hilda and Theol, on their high-wire act. Two of the sisters, Rosina and Hilda, also hit the big time in 1928, when they performed with Lon Chaney in the movie *Laugh, Clown, Laugh*. Hilda Nelson doubled for actress Loretta Young on a high-wire act while her sister Rosina doubled for actress Sissy Fitzgerald. Several years later, while performing with the Sparks Circus, the sisters learned of the death of famous actor Lon Chaney at the age of forty-seven. "A wonderful actor, a friend and at all times a gentleman" was the brief comment the Nelsons made to an Alabama newspaper.

The family also had their share of tragedies. Perhaps one of the saddest was the death of Hilda Nelson's young daughter in 1928. Five people were killed and five injured when a pair of taxicabs collided with a train in Saskatchewan, Canada; young June Nelson Arneil was seated on her mother's lap and killed on impact. Members of the family were performing in the local fair circuit and were traveling to town after a performance when their taxi ran into Canadian National engine on its way to a local train yard. Another taxi, riding behind the one carrying the Nelsons, also ran into the train. Newspaper accounts at the time further stated that the taxicab "was smashed to bits," and Hilda Nelson was bleeding profusely and hysterical. An inquest following the incident found the cab driver should have used more caution and gates needed to be installed near the train tracks. June was the toddler daughter of Hilda and Thomas Arneil, a real estate agent, and her body was returned to Mount Clemens for burial.

The Nelson family continued to work as circus performers into the late 1930s. In addition to Sparks Circus, they performed with Sells-Floto Circus and the Cole Bros.–Clyde Beatty Circus. In 1969, the Nelsons were among six different performing groups to receive the circus's highest honor when they were inducted into the Circus Hall of Fame in Sarasota, Florida.

THOMAS EDISON

Inventor's Namesake No Genius

The light bulb, the telephone and the phonograph are among Thomas Alva Edison's many inventions, but the fact that the Mount Clemens native actually received 1,093 patents in his lifetime is both impressive and interesting. He counts several waterproofing, rubber and insulating compounds on a long list of accomplishments.

Edison was born in Ohio in 1847, the seventh child of Samuel and Nancy Edison. When he was seven years old, his family moved to Port Huron, Michigan. Surprisingly, Edison had very little formal education; instead, his mother taught him reading and arithmetic, but he remained distracted and curious about the world around him. He left home at thirteen and took a job as a newsboy selling newspapers on the local railroad that ran from Port Huron to Detroit.

When Edison was fifteen, he was working in the train station in Mount Clemens, and one day, he saved three-year-old Jimmy Mackenzie from a runaway freight car. The station's telegraph operator was the boy's father,

Exterior view of the Grand Trunk Railway station at Mount Clemens, located off Cass Avenue at the Grand Trunk tracks. The brick depot was built in 1859 when the railroad line running from Port Huron to Detroit came through Mount Clemens. *Mount Clemens Library Collection.*

and he was so grateful he trained Edison in telegraphy, which launched his interest in technology. As he grew more interested in experiments and electricity, Edison moved on to New York and Indiana, working in small makeshift laboratories, some in the basements of friends' home, as he wasn't making much money.

Edison was married twice, the first time at the age of twenty-four to sixteen-year-old Mary Stillwell, and they had three children: Marion, Thomas Jr. and William. When Stillwell died at twenty-nine, Edison remarried two years later to twenty-year-old Mina Miller, and they had three more children: Madeline, Charles and Theodore. Up to his eyeballs in laboratory experiments, Edison was a somewhat absent father. It appears that his two eldest children, nicknamed Dot and Dash, got the most attention, although it wasn't always positive. An intellectual who never ceased reading, writing and asking questions, Edison would quiz his children at the breakfast table and scold them if they failed to answer his questions correctly. A blurb in a daily newspaper in 1890 described the inventor as beyond obsessed, "so absorbed in his work is he that he frequently forgets to take his meals or go to bed. He spends ten to twelve hours in his laboratory without tasting food and sleeping in his chair."

As it turned out, his eldest daughter, "Dot," was quite intelligent and witty and, had she not been a woman, could have earnestly followed in her father's footsteps into the lab and the record books. Instead, Dot was an outspoken Republican who ran for Congress in 1938, strongly supported Red Cross blood drives in Indiana during World War II and took charge of overseeing the museum in Ohio that honors her father's birthplace.

Unfortunately, Edison's firstborn son and namesake did not respond well to the pressures of having a famous father. He dropped out of school and was unsuccessful in creating his own inventions, so he got involved with unsavory individuals in get-rich-quick schemes. Banking on the Edison name, Tom Jr. was taking out large advertisements in local publications and touting a liquid that was a miracle cure for everything from back pain to menstrual cramps. Shocked by his son's turn in life, Edison Sr. soon took him to court in 1903 to halt the use of his good name. A local paper reported the case was the most "peculiar" the court had seen, as Edison Sr. asked that a judgment be made against the Edison Chemical Company out of Delaware, which was claiming he was directly involved in the products being sold. In reality, it was his son who was involved in the hoax.

Edison Sr. further stated that he was publicly known by the nickname "the wizard" due to the successes of his inventions and numerous patents, and his

Thomas Edison. *Library of Congress.*

son's firm was placing that moniker on all its products—further defaming his good name. Edison Jr. testified that he was given $5,000 worth of stock and $5 a month from Edison Chemical Company for the use of his name and that recently changed to $10 a week and a 5 percent stock dividend once a year. He admitted he had not invented any of the products his company was selling. An injunction was granted against the use of the Edison name later that year, and Edison Sr. agreed to pay his son a $35 a week allowance if he would change his name. Edison Jr. did and was known as Thomas Willard for a time.

Still, his troubles weren't over. A substance abuse problem, mainly alcohol, was Edison Jr.'s next demon, and it led him back to court in 1921. He went before a judge on the charge of turning his washing machine into a still and the wringer into a wine press. A raid of his home-produced bottles of a dark-colored liquid, mushed raisins in the bottom of the washing machine and red stains on the clothes wringer. A test of the dark liquid revealed it was a beverage that packed quite the wallop at 44 percent alcohol. Edison Jr., who was arrested under the name John Cooper, told the judge he squeezed the life out of the raisins by running them through the

Thomas Edison Jr. *Library of Congress.*

wringer, which was quite upsetting to his wife, because the residue left stains on all their clothing. "Thomas Edison Jr., I fine you $200 and sixty days in the workhouse," was the judge's response to his antics.

An electrical show in New York several years later revealed Edison Jr. had a somewhat soft side: he halted a waffle eating contest after a boy consumed eighteen—he didn't want him to come to any harm. It was on this occasion that Edison Jr. perhaps inadvertently gave a brief glimpse into his childhood. He noted that it was nice to see all his father's inventions displayed again, as he had observed many in the family home in 1879 when he was just six years old. As a retort, an agent of his father who was at the exhibit, said his recollection was that Edison Jr. and his sister used to steal all the lab beakers to make mud pies and would break the lamps just to hear them pop. "Many experiments you nearly ruined," scolded the man, shedding light on how perhaps Edison Jr.'s upbringing was fraught with criticism. Edison Jr. was married twice, had no children, spent time in a sanatorium and died at the age of fifty-nine.

In contrast, Thomas Edison Sr. knew great wealth and fame for the bulk of his life and brought numerous inventions to the world that we can all still appreciate today. A man of many wise words—here's a quote from the world-renowned inventor:

> *There is no substitute for hard work. Just because something doesn't do what you planned it to do doesn't mean it's useless. If we did all the things, we are capable of, we would literally astound ourselves.*

Victor Wertz

Baseball, Beer and a Very Big Heart

Professional baseball player, World War II veteran, major beer distributor and an active philanthropist in his community are all roles Vic Wertz held, most of them tied to his life in Mount Clemens.

Victor Woodrow Wertz was born in Pennsylvania in 1925 and was a left-handed first baseman drafted by the Detroit Tigers in 1942. Instead of taking to the dugout, he went into military service first, returning to play ball in 1947. In all, Wertz played seventeen years in the major leagues, including time with the Detroit Tigers, St. Louis Browns, Baltimore Orioles, Cleveland Indians, Boston Red Sox and Minnesota Twins. He was named an American League All-Star four times and played in the 1954 World Series on the Cleveland Indians roster. In that game, he hit the long fly ball on which outfielder Willie Mays made his famous over-the shoulder catch, 450 feet to the center field wall. After he retired, Wertz kept a photo of "The Catch" on the office wall at his beer distribution company because he had no regrets about the event.

Wertz told United Press International in 1979,

> *I'm very proud that I'm associated with it. I look at it this way: If that ball Willie caught had been a home run or a triple, how many people would've remembered me? Not many. This way, everybody who meets me for the first time always identifies me with Willie's catch, and that makes me feel good.*

One major blip in his athletic career hit Wertz in 1955. He came down with what was initially thought to be a forty-eight-hour flu bug, but as his temperature soared and severe pain set in, it turned out to be an attack of polio. Luckily, it was the non-paralysis kind. After being bedridden for weeks and losing twenty pounds, Wertz began to walk again while building up his strength. He received fourteen thousand get well letters, most from children, and returned to spring training in 1956. He finished his baseball career in September 1963 with the Minnesota Twins.

After baseball, Wertz was still well known for his charming personality and lack of hair—yes, baldness was a personal trait. He married Bernice Wineka early in his career, and they had two children, Terence and Patricia. Their marriage ended in the early 1950s, and in 1952, Vic married Lucille Caroll Caleel; they had no children.

Left: Baseball player Victor Wertz with President Dwight D. Eisenhower. *Courtesy of Ashley Wertz.*

Below: Victor Wertz at his wedding to his second wife, Lucille Caroll Caleel, in 1952. Detroit Tigers pitcher Hal Newhouser and his wife look on. *Courtesy of Ashley Wertz.*

Vic Wertz owned a beer distribution company in Mount Clemens and also was a collector of classic cars, several of which are pictured here. *Courtesy of Ashley Wertz.*

Looking beyond his baseball career, Wertz invested in a small beer distribution company in Mount Clemens in 1955, and upon his retirement from the major leagues, he went from baseball to brews, turning the company into a multimillion-dollar success.

Good deeds were also high on Wertz's to-do-list. He was known to visit young fans who suffered from polio, to give them encouragement, mindful of his own good fortune after he had such a close call with the disease. Supporting local charities like Easter Seals, the March of Dimes and the local Boys and Girls Club were also important to the retired ball player. He hosted an annual golf outing for the Boys and Girls Club that raised $350,000.

A collector of vintage Rolls Royces and the occasional Thunderbird convertible, Wertz regularly loaned the cars out for use in local parades. When he decided to try snowmobiling in 1981, a new hobby was born. Within a year, Wertz had created Wertz Warriors, a group that would make an annual snowmobile trek across the state of Michigan to raise money for the Special Olympics.

Wertz only made two trips to fundraise for those in need aboard his snowmobile; despite his untimely death in 1983 at the age of fifty-eight during heart surgery, the Wertz Warriors carried on. It was a shocking end to the life of a man who had done so much for the community. Over three decades, the group has raised nearly $9 million to support the State Winter Games for Special Olympic athletes in Wertz's memory.

All that philanthropy reflects Wertz's giving heart, as does a story shared about him by Detroit sportswriter Joe Falls in a column following the baseball player's death. New on the baseball beat, Falls wrote that he was covering a Tigers opening day in St. Louis in 1953, nervous and not wanting to bring attention to himself, when suddenly someone said, "Hey you're Joe Falls aren't you?" It was Wertz, now playing for the St. Louis Cardinals, and he quickly took Falls around and introduced him to the all the other players, saying "Hey, say hello to my friend, Joe Falls. He's a writer from Detroit." What a way to break into the major leagues. Falls said, "It was one of the great acts of kindness that I ever knew."

7

Richmond

The community was founded in 1835 by Erastus Beebe on land located on the eastern border of Macomb County, with a small portion falling into western St. Clair County. He arrived in the wilderness and began platting land that would become Beebe Corners. In 1859, the Grand Trunk Railway opened, providing easy access to the area's lumber and agricultural products. As the industry flourished by 1878, the voters of Beebe's Corners and the two neighboring communities, Ridgeway and Cooper Town, agreed to incorporate as one community. The following year, by an act of the Michigan legislature, the Village of Richmond was born. In 1966, Richmond was officially incorporated as a city. The city covers just under three miles and today has a population of six thousand.

GILBERT EDISON MILLER

Mr. "Square Deal" Had Jackrabbits, Snakes and Discount Eggs

As a boy growing up in Richmond, Gilbert Miller first envisioned a career as a banker, but after spending time working every day after school at a local bank and earning six dollars a month, he decided it was not to be his profession. He asked how could it be, as he had a round face that liked to smile, and most bankers have long solemn mugs.

Next, he thought perhaps his dream of being an actor would pan out: he was already a cornet player and an advance man and could perform tricks on his bicycle. Alas, that career seemed to begin and end in one quick summer, but he did meet Albert Kuldt, the only other person in Richmond with a bicycle. Kuldt also owned a jewelry store. It seems the meeting of the two was quite fortuitous, because Kuldt was offered a job with a jeweler in Detroit and sold his shop to Miller and his father.

Miller, who was born in Richmond in 1876 to Albert and Elsie Miller, graduated from Richmond High School and married Maude Yeaton. In 1897, they had a son, Earl Don Miller. After working in his hometown for a number of years, Miller opened his own jewelry shop in Detroit in 1904. It was a tiny space, just six by twenty feet, but his business grew rapidly. In fact, Miller credited the small space for making him even more determined to find unique ways to advertise and bring in more customers.

He decided to build his customer base by offering exceptional deals and impeccable service with a 99 percent refund policy on all diamonds sold. Soon he came up with the moniker "Square Deal Miller." A typical one-line ad in the early days might say, "The biggest little store on Grand River, open evenings with everything the big stores have but the expense." Miller's technique paid off at an incredible pace, and within a decade, he had opened a thirty-thousand-square-foot store that employed over fifty and earned over $1 million annually. His unusual personality, quick wit and ability to make friends with literally everyone who crossed his path didn't hurt either.

Some of Miller's signature tag lines included:

> *Square Deal means I'd rather hand a customer his money back than have him dissatisfied.*
> *They say I can't sell at my prices and live....I'll let you know when to send flowers.*
> *If I'm on top of the ladder of success you can bet I didn't land there—I climbed there.*

Some of his gimmicks were legendary. Once, eggs were selling for sixty cents a dozen at the grocery store, so he advertised his at thirty-eight cents a dozen, limit 2 dozen per customer, fully fresh and guaranteed to be in perfect condition, like his jewelry. There was such a rush at his store for the eggs that six police officers were called in to handle the crowd and all 1,900 dozen were sold in just fifty-one minutes. Another time, citing the high cost of meat, he advertised fresh-killed alfalfa and wheat-fed rabbits for sale at

Photograph No. 254
Gilbert "Square Deal" Miller.
Town clock donor.
The clock was dedicated July 17,
1924.

Gilbert "Square Deal" Miller posed with one of the snakes he was fond of giving to people. *The Lois Wagner Memorial Library Historical Photo Collection.*

his shop for six cents a pound. The tagline was, "Selling meat is out of my line but butchering high prices has been my profession for years." These approaches to customer service may not have paid off directly on the days the eggs and rabbits were purchased, but customers remembered him and his store for years to come. He also had special pens and pads of paper bearing his Square Deal Miller moniker delivered to hundreds of local traffic cops as a thank-you for sending customers his way.

An avid hunter, Miller gained some national notoriety in 1915 when he shot a white deer in Northern Michigan, the first of its kind bagged in some twenty-five years. The popular jeweler admitted he initially thought he'd shot a rabbit but, when he went to recover his kill, realized it was a white deer. He was a Mason, an Elk and a Moose over the years, but his affinity for giving snakes as gifts drew plenty of attention.

An article in the *Port Huron Times Herald* in 1937 reported that Miller had presented officers with the Michigan State Police in St. Clair with a Florida king snake. The three-foot reptile was living in a screened-in box on the roof of the police garage as officers made plans to feed it a steady supply of mice and frogs. The nonvenomous snake was said to be capable of developing great affection for anyone who treated it kindly. Next, Square Deal Miller donated a snake pit and a collection of reptiles to the Detroit Zoo. Again, the reptiles' arrival was met with some surprise by zoo director John T. Miller, but he had to admit attendance at the exhibit was plentiful.

Fortunately, when it came to presenting a gift to his hometown, Miller kept the reptiles away, and in 1924, he donated a beautiful cast-iron clock statue with four faces. It was installed at North Main and Park Streets. Calling it a testimonial of his affection for his birthplace, the community quickly made the clock a fixture in the city, adding it to official stationery and logos—even adopting the tagline "a city with time for you." There have been a few repairs to the clock over the years, but it remains in place today.

Miller eventually turned his business over to his son, Earl, and retired. Then, in 1949, the headlines blared from local papers when Square Deal Miller died at the age of seventy-three. Noting that he once sold jackrabbits with his jewelry, his obituary said he started his business with $700 and a knack for slogans, boosting his business into one of the largest jewelry houses in the state. In his will, he left his entire estate to his son, Earl, valued at more than $10,000 and more than $150,000 in personal property.

In a strange footnote to a family story that had seemingly enjoyed only successes in life, in June 1961, Miller's grandson and namesake, Gilbert Miller, thirty, was shot and killed by his friend of twenty years, Gerald Hollerbach, thirty-one, who said he thought Miller was a prowler. The incident occurred in Hollerbach's parents' home in Grosse Pointe Park. He told the police that he was sleeping when he heard someone walking out of his bedroom, so he grabbed his shotgun. He followed the intruder downstairs and shot him twice. Miller, who had been separated from his wife, Jeanne

Gilbert Miller seated in his car with his family around him. *The Lois Wagner Memorial Library Historical Photo Collection.*

Wright Miller, for about six months and was living with his mother nearby, was found on a sofa. His jacket was discovered on the kitchen floor, with Hollerbach's house keys and a wallet inside a pocket. News reports stated that after a brief investigation there was not enough evidence to indicate a crime had occurred. The case was closed, but six months later, in January 1962, Hollerbach made the front page of the local newspaper once again. He and the widow Miller had gotten married and remained so for more than thirty years.

THE CITY POOL

Pool Born of Tragedy Still a Summer Staple

When two twelve-year-old boys drowned in a local pond in 1966, they were added to a shocking list of lost swimmers in the city. In fact, ten children drowned in ponds and rivers over a nine-year period. After the double tragedy that took the lives of Robert P. Blake and Arthur D. Dreim, the community devised a plan to keep local swimmers safe by launching the Blake Dreim Memorial Swimming Pool Fund.

When the local newspaper of record, the *Richmond Review* kept the funding drive front and center that summer, a board of pool trustees and a bank account were quickly established, as a plan began to take shape. The board included Chairman Rosemary Scott, Vice Chairman Harold McNinch, Treasurer Eugene Jakubiak and Secretary Sandy Dewar. The first fundraiser for the pool was a dance for teens at the Richmond High School Gym. It was also noted that the City of Richmond had $22,000 in recreation funds that it would give to the campaign.

Dr. Patrick McClellan, who served on the first pool committee and still lives in the city, recalled how the drowning of the two young boys provided serious provocation for him to get involved in providing a pool in the community. He had just been named a deputy to the county medical examiner serving northern Macomb County, and as it happened, his very first task was to perform the autopsy for one of the boys who drowned in the pond. He recalled it had a profound effect on him.

The reaction of the community was equally strong, and the pool project became a huge team effort, including strong support from the city although no one person was any more instrumental in getting the job done than any other. McClellan does recall that fellow pool committee member and local business owner Jim Weeks made a substantial donation to the pool fund at the start, and a room full of organizers fell silent at his generosity. Things took off from that point, and in addition to a growing fund, skilled tradespeople in the community donated their time, their tools and their skills to the project.

Still, there were plenty of hoops to jump through once the funding was in place. It took two years, including concerns for safety, sanitation and the standards the architects needed to meet. There were some stops and starts as the bugs got worked out, but the team mentality remained in place. McClellan recalled how one contractor was making his way to the city with a truckload of sand for back filling the pool area and he was stopped by the weight master on the freeway because he was over the limit. Instead of a ticket, the sand driver got a police escort to the pool area—that's how strongly the project affected everyone in the area.

It was decided that the pool would be placed in the city's Beebe Street Park, and the city administration would be in charge of it going forward. The pool was formally dedicated in 1968.

While the idea of a communal pool has gone by the wayside in most communities today, Richmond's city pool has remained an important part of the summer for decades. It's a recreation resource for families and a safe environment to teach youth to swim. The pool opens for swimming lessons,

Dedication of the Richmond City Pool in 1968. *The Lois Wagner Memorial Library Historical Photo Collection.*

open swims and water aerobics programs from mid-June to late August and is also available for rental. Residents and nonresidents can enjoy the facilities, including the pool, locker rooms, poolside chairs and picnic tables.

Looking back, McClellan said, it was several years from the start of the fundraisers until the pool became a reality, but it's something he will never forget. He noted that he was fortunate enough to be on a high school football team that won a state championship, and while that was memorable, being part of the pool project ranks right up there too.

A pool committee reunion was held poolside in 2018. McClellan offered a moment of silence for those who were lost and prompted the city's decision to construct the pool plus recognize anyone who was involved in making it happen but were unable to attend. The inaugural pool director, Don Rettke, and resident Jim Weeks were also in attendance. Weeks, who donated the initial dollars to start the pool project, said the committee did not want recognition. Instead, he said, it was important to remember they launched the pool plan for a good reason.

The fiftieth anniversary of the opening of the Richmond City Pool, including original committee members James Weeks and Patrick McClellan. *The Lois Wagner Memorial Historical Photo Collection.*

The recreational opportunity has had a major effect on the community over the last fifty years, providing swimming lessons to thousands of children and a place to simply cool off in the summer.

LIBRARIAN LOIS WAGNER

A Beloved Bookworm

When Lois Wagner logged a record fifty-year career at the Richmond Library, many felt that if not for ill health, she could have easily put in another twenty years at the helm.

A lifelong city resident, Wagner was born in December 1926 to Frederick and Gertrude Wagner, who owned and operated the local movie house in town. She had three siblings, two sisters and a brother. She utilized crutches from the time she was twelve years old after suffering a bout of polio and graduated from St. Augustine Catholic High School in 1945 in a wheelchair. She was in the last class to graduate from Port Huron Junior College in 1952 before it became St. Clair County Community College. She earned as associate degree in art.

Wagner began her career at the library at the age of twenty, and the facility already had quite a history. The first public library in Richmond was actually started at the home of Olney Culver, who opened her parlor to the public in 1912. The library was founded by the ladies of the Civic Society, and when it outgrew the parlor, it moved to the Chaffee Building downtown. Then, in 1936, the library took over the second floor of the Civic Auditorium. That location was short-lived, and it moved to the Buer Funeral Home in 1967. In 1974, it moved off of Main Street for the first time, to its current location off Division Road, where, in 1992, an addition that doubled the floor space was completed.

Lois Wagner's high school graduation photo from the class of 1945 at St. Augustine Catholic High School. *The Lois Wagner Memorial Library Historical Photo Collection.*

Wagner actually worked at three library locations, starting out at the Civic Auditorium. In fact, the city council was concerned about naming her the librarian since the facility was located on the second floor of the auditorium, but she managed without a problem. Friends and patrons said that they knew Wagner was in pain much of the time, but she never mentioned it or complained.

In a rare newspaper interview, Wagner once talked about her condition. She recalled that the disease produced a high fever, and when the fever ended, her muscles were shot. She said her personality didn't allow for self-pity, but at times, she did get disgusted about not being able to do things that others could do with ease. She said she never had a hard time getting a job due to her handicap and had several clerk-typist posts at local businesses before going to work at the city librarian. Wagner said the opportunity came about when the previous librarian resigned. They were friends, so she just kind of picked up the post and kept going. It was a part-time job at first, so she also worked in the accounting department at city hall.

Lois Wagner was also an avid community volunteer, acting as the business manager for the Richmond Community Theatre, one of nine executive board members for the city's Good Old Days Festival and a strong supporter of Boy Scout Troop 84. She also wrote a column for several local newspapers about the goings-on in town. Still, described as modest and not one to take

Lois Wagner poses with the library sign bearing her name. *The Lois Wagner Memorial Library Historical Photo Collection.*

credit for her accomplishments, Wagner's main goal was getting everyone interested in books.

The twenty-fifth anniversary of Wagner's time at the library was recognized with an open house sponsored by the library board. She was referred to as a legend in her own time due to her friendly personality and winning smile despite her disability. At the time, Wagner said she read one hundred books a year and hoped to write one of her own someday. A romantic, she once said she planned to a write a romance novel with the heroine being a librarian, of course. She also had childhood dreams of being a movie star and did have several roles on stage at the Richmond Community Theatre.

Wagner passed away in April 1998 at the age of seventy-one, following complications from a stroke. A plan to name the library in her honor, which was to be a surprise for her, went forward, and today the Richmond Library is known as the Lois Wagner Memorial Library. Longtime coworker and library technical assistant Colleen Kelley couldn't wait to see Wagner's face at the renaming of the library.

We were going to surprise her with it, I'm sure she would have protested it, but I think it was the best possible thing they could do, and it's a tribute to her that was very well deserved. Lois was such a positive influence on adults and young people that after she passed away there was a fear that things would change at the library or that spirit of community would go away, but it hasn't.

In a newspaper article celebrating the 100th anniversary of the library in 2012, Mayor Tim Rix described his childhood librarian and longtime friend as a real character who was funny and warm and had the Dick Clark look—she never aged. He added that the only time her sweet demeanor would dim would be when she needed something for the library, and she'd beg, borrow and steal to get it.

Current librarian Julianne Kammer has memories of working alongside Wagner, though Kammer was a mere eight-year-old at the time. She used to pack her brown bag lunch and go to the library to do volunteer work for Wagner and Kelley.

Today, Wagner's legacy remains in many aspects of the library; in fact, she had so many positive sayings she'd share with staff they have a list of them at the front desk, including "Onward and Upward" and "Carry On."

Wagner once admitted she couldn't do a lot of things because of her handicap, but she was fortunate to have friends to help her get along. As for the city she called home all of her life, she simply said, "I grew up here, and I love it." The feeling was certainly mutual.

8

Romeo

The Village of Romeo is situated at the southeast corner of Bruce Township, with a portion extending south into Washington Township. In the mid-1800s, it had mills and carriage factories, making it one of the biggest manufacturers in the county, and was a place where wealthy landowners purchased lots or property even if they lived somewhere else. The first village lot sold for twelve dollars around 1835, and within a couple of years, there were three grocery stores, shoe shops, a foundry and a hoopskirt factory. Originally known as Hoxies Settlement, in 1838, the village was incorporated. At the turn of the century, an Opera House and Cultural Center brought several thousand people to town on the weekends. The village maintained its small-town charm and historic sites for decades, and in 1971, it was named a National and State Historic District. Today, the village covers just over two miles and has a population of 3,600.

AMANDA MOORE

Daughter of Slaves' Rescued Children

The idea of taking in and caring for Black children sent her way by charitable organizations, including the Children's Aid Society of Detroit, wasn't something Amanda Moore planned when she moved to Romeo in 1898.

Born in 1868 in Petersburg, Virginia, to parents who had once been enslaved, Moore was the youngest of fourteen children. After being orphaned at ten, she faced many hard times, working as a field hand for five cents day and a seamstress before moving to Michigan as a servant for a family heading north.

In 1905, she pooled her savings to purchase a ramshackle home on Hollister Street. She soon became the area's most popular caterer, and no party could be complete without Moore and "her girls" at the helm. Her assistance behind the scenes became a status symbol in the community.

By 1919, the house was known as "Miss Moore's" place. Dozens of children, some with health problems, special needs and the ones others couldn't manage rode the streetcar to Moore's small white frame home. Some remained there for a decade and others just weeks, but all left with Moore's lessons of discipline, courage and love.

Former child tenant Marie Clark recalled how she and her two sisters were taken in by Moore following the death of their mother. When the young sisters started school, Moore was lonely at home, and that's when she took

Amanda Moore with her adopted and foster children at her ninety-fifth birthday celebration in 1963. *From the* Macomb Daily.

in her first foster child, with the number quickly growing to ten children. Seeing Moore, a person of minimal means, work so hard to give so much is something Clark carried with her into adulthood.

By 1949, Moore was an honored member of the Romeo community and was named the city's Mother of the Year. In all, Moore mothered ninety-three girls and sixty-three boys, and countless other children, aged five weeks to seventeen years, passed through her doors, if even for a few hours. She kept a box of toys beneath her kitchen table for young visitors, and her home was renovated over the years to a six-room frame house with modern facilities before it was closed as a boardinghouse in 1954.

In 1963, a large group of Romeo residents gathered to honor Moore on her ninety-fifth birthday. Friends collected photos and cards into a scrapbook for her to admire, and she kept it close until a virus just a month after her ninety-sixth birthday took her life.

When Moore passed away in March 1964 hundreds of people phoned, wrote and wired notes from as far away as Los Angeles with many more filing past her casket to pay their respects. Marion Hood, who spent twenty years as one of Ms. Moore's children, was quoted in a local newspaper following the funeral:

> *She was a mother to me. I never thought of her as a foster parent. There were no legal ties, but it was love that kept it together.*

Harry MacDonald, who spent a year at Moore's Romeo home, added:

> *She taught me not to run away. I was one of the hard-to-handle ones. She taught me the first day who was boss and then she taught me to settle down.*

In 1971, the Romeo School District built the Amanda Moore School, now Amanda Moore Elementary School, in her honor.

FRANKLIN HAROLD HAYWARD

Traded Family Life for Art Studio

The famous oil painting *Whistler's Mother*, created by American-born artist James McNeill Whistler in 1871, is worth $30 million today which likely wouldn't surprise artist Franklin Harold Hayward, who spent two years in

Portrait of Mount Clemens artist Franklin Harold Hayward. Hayward was born in Romeo, Michigan, in 1867. *From the Macomb Daily.*

Paris under Whistler's tutelage, an experience he called priceless. Calling his former teacher one of the greatest masters of all time, Hayward, who was born in Romeo but grew up in Mount Clemens, became a highly respected painter and sculptor in his own right—although some would claim he traded his family life for his art studio.

Hayward was born in 1867 to Abner and Alice Hayward in Romeo, and the family moved to Mount Clemens when he was four years old. The Haywards were both doctors during the Civil War, and Alice was one of the first female physicians in the state of Michigan. Abner was a well-known local practitioner who often told his patients suffering from rheumatism to use the baths at the famous bathhouses in Mount Clemens. Despite the couple's professional success, tales of their arguing and ornery personalities were well known in the community at the time. One sore point was the fact that Alice brought substantial wealth to the marriage. Abner wanted to use the money as he saw fit, and she objected. She actually took him to court to prevent the dissolution of her bank accounts. Even though women were mostly considered the property of their spouses back then, she won the case. Sadly, that just increased the distrust between them, which made it a difficult household to grow up in for Franklin and his sister, Maude. In fact, in later years, Franklin's own daughter and granddaughter attributed his horrid attitude, particularly toward women, as a result of the harrowing atmosphere he grew up in.

An avid artist from a young age, Franklin was known to create impressive charcoal and crayon portraits while still a teenager. He was just seventeen when he opened his own studio in downtown Mount Clemens, and in 1886, he won two first prizes for an exhibition of his work at the Michigan State Fair. Franklin graduated from Mount Clemens High School in 1884 and went on to the Chicago Art Institute to study. He returned to Michigan in 1898 to marry Olive Bell Hull, who came from a well-to-do family from Albion. A newspaper clipping from the day read: "The happy pair will spend a few days at Niagara, will take a trip down the St. Lawrence, and, after August 20th will be at home to their friends at the Hotel du Louvre,

Paris, France." The couple used her dowry to move to Paris so he could pursue his career as an artist. It was there that he spent several years studying under Whistler while gaining recognition for his paintings at large public exhibitions. His paintings were selected to hang in museums in both Paris and England while exhibitions featuring his work made their way to galleries across the United States.

In a letter to his mother from Paris in 1900, Hayward wrote:

Many of the most prominent American artists have adopted Paris as their home, which is not a cause of wonderment when we breathe the atmosphere which pervades the place and is necessary for its existence. It has been the effort of France to make Paris first and to encourage art in all ways. On entering Paris, the artist finds himself surrounded by every object which can delight and interest his imagination. Here an air of art pervades and one is loath to turn away

Despite that flowery description of his European home, the Haywards' decision to return to Michigan came after Olive suffered the loss of their first child in France; when she became pregnant with their second, she demanded they return home for its birth.

They sailed in 1901, and their daughter Olive Belle was born in Mount Clemens; her only sibling, Alice Louise, came along several years later, in 1904. Hayward opened an art studio in downtown Mount Clemens, where he was a teacher, illustrator, sculptor and portrait painter. He soon became famous for his portraits of dignitaries in Europe and at home, including his oil canvases featuring local governors.

Meanwhile, at home, Hayward was alleged to have been quite the tyrant. His eldest daughter later recalled her fear over what might happen to her mother at her father's hand. When she was fifteen years old, she came home to find her mother dead on their front porch, her father out of town on business. Another shocking revelation was that Hayward is alleged to have been tossing his younger daughter up in the air when he failed to catch her, and she smashed her head on a metal sewing machine. She recovered physically but spent the remainder of her life in an institution with brain damage. Following the death of her mother, Olive spent several rough years at home with her father before meeting her future husband, Watson Ball, in 1919 and eloping to Texas. She never spoke to her father again.

As Franklin remained in Mount Clemens, toiling away in his art studio, he suffered great hardships and monetary losses during the Depression but

Interior view of the art studio of Franklin Harold Hayward (1867–1945), which was located at 24 New Street in Mount Clemens. *From the* Macomb Daily.

remained devoted to his canvas. In an interview in 1931, he stated that he was always studying and would always be a student and didn't want to be anything else. Apparently, that was a good thing, because he never even met the three grandchildren his daughter Olive had and raised out West. They weren't even allowed to ask about their grandparents according to his youngest granddaughter, Josephine Anderson, who penned a biography of the Hayward family revealing the intimate details of her own mother's upbringing. She claimed her mother, Olive, had an abiding hate for the man. Anderson actually attained her own notoriety when she started the women's group, Renewing Love, which practiced Christian-based living. It grew to include chapters in thirteen countries on three continents with over sixty thousand members. She passed away in 1996 after a long battle with cancer. As to the world-famous grandfather she never met, well, as Hayward closed in on his own demise, he remained an artist in dire circumstances, barely getting by with help from friends. In one of his last reported interviews, he said, "I want to work until the last hour that I live." He died in 1945 at the age of seventy-eight. He completed over one hundred works of art in his lifetime, and many still hang in state capitols, museums and halls of justice across America.

9

Shelby Township

Shelby Township was first surveyed and opened for general land sales in 1818, and the township government was established in 1827. The township included what is now the city of Sterling Heights until 1835, when that area, then known as Jefferson Township, separated from Shelby.

One of the nation's most ambitious canal projects, the Clinton-Kalamazoo Canal, runs through the township. The settlement of Disco, platted in 1849 but never formally incorporated as its own municipality, was also part of the township and was prosperous in its day with an academy for students and a post office. The Packard Motor Car Company opened in 1927, and in the 1930s, world heavyweight boxing champion Joe Louis bought Spring Hill Farm, 250 acres he turned into a horse farm. Shelby Township includes just over 35 square miles and a population of seventy-four thousand.

COLONEL ALONZO KEELER

Infamous Educator, Soldier, Public Servant

Farmer, teacher, soldier, principal, administrator of the church and register of deeds for Macomb County—the list of achievements seems to go on and on for Shelby Township pioneer Alonzo Keeler. John and Mary Fellows

Keeler, his parents, moved to Washington Township in 1826 with their infant son and settled on a farm there. Alonzo was homeschooled for a time, and then he pursued his education in Rochester and in Oberlin, Ohio, to prepare for a career in teaching. At twenty-one, he took on his first teaching post in a one-room schoolhouse and, at twenty-three, took a bride, marrying Lucy A. Church on New Year's Eve 1849. They had six children over the next seventeen years, four sons and two daughters.

In 1849, he was named the principal at Disco Academy in Shelby Township, serving in that post from 1850 to 1856. According to state education records, the plan to build the school in Disco took shape in 1849 under the direction of Keeler, and when it opened a year later, he took charge. The accommodations were rustic at best in a building constructed with tamarack logs, slabs for student seating, a desk for the teacher and a small stove for heat. Keeler had to make and mend goosequill pens and make the ink from the bark of soft maple and butternut trees. Collecting his pay was equally primitive, as he had to go door-to-door and the rates were based solely upon the daily attendance of each pupil. Students clamored to attend the new school, traveling from nearby towns, and state records reflect it was one of the most popular schools in the state. Several years along, the school was formally named Disco Academy, derived from the Latin *disco*, which means "to learn." A former student and educator at the school recalled that it was a privilege to attend the school in those days and students were eager to learn. The academy continued on as a school until it became obsolete, and in 1865, it was made a public school, losing the academy moniker. A decade later, a new public school was constructed, and the old building became a meeting hall and storage place behind the new school. Keeler's career in the classroom continued beyond the academy. He went to teach in nearby Rochester for a year, followed by teaching in the first old brick school building in Utica, and he also taught the first term at the new building for several years.

In 1862, as the Civil War took hold, Keeler, thirty-six, left his students behind and enlisted in Company B, Twenty-Second Michigan Volunteer Infantry Company, gathering 115 men in five days to leave behind their farms and families to join him on the fighting lines. They elected him captain before he was taken prisoner and spent eighteen months in jails in Macon, Georgia, and Richmond Virginia. Excerpts from letters Keeler sent home while he was a prisoner were gathered by Robert and Cheryl Allen, authors of the book *A Guest of the Confederacy*.

Keeler wrote:

> *We slept on our line without blankets and nearly without rations—heavy frost—At 9 o'clock we were ordered to march to reinforce Gen. Thomas—from 1 to 2 p.m. we were brought out against the rebel Gen. Preston—The 22 was engaged in the most horrific fire for four hours—We lost heavily in killed and wounded and were all taken prisoners.*

> *A cool morning—foggy—heavy dew—poor soil—pine and persimmons about from Georgia to Virginia. Arrived at Wilton at 8:30 a.m. change cars for Petersburg. Arrive at Petersburg at 4 p.m. Arrive at Richmond and take up our abode in Libby Prison at 8 p.m. This in 10 days is a wonderful change—Now we cannot step on sacred soil for the Old Dominion—When shall we be free gain.*

An interesting note regarding Keeler's time in the Libby Prison in Richmond was the fact that he was said to be among more than one hundred men who escaped captivity through an underground tunnel in 1864. The tunnel was dug using chisels and wooden spittoons in a rat-infested area beneath their overcrowded cells infrequently visited by the prison guards. The Union prisoners spent seventeen days digging the tunnel behind a stove, traveling fifty to sixty feet in spots that sometimes were just sixteen inches wide, all while fighting off hungry rats. The tunnel led to a small building near the gates to the jail that were also not often in the guards' sights. They thought the prison was escape-proof. It was reported that fifty-nine soldiers survived and rejoined their regiments, two drowned crossing a nearby river and forty-eight were recaptured. A story in the *Detroit Free Press* in January 1900 on the occasion of Keeler's fiftieth wedding anniversary noted his role in the prison break. After leaving the prison camp, Keeler reentered active service and was promoted to major in early 1865 and afterward to colonel on July 12, 1865, before returning home to begin teaching again.

In 1868, he was elected register of deeds for Macomb County, serving for one term, and he is credited with creating an abstract

Colonel Alonzo Keeler. *Courtesy of the Utica Heritage Association.*

of the county that was considered very valuable work. Then, in 1875, Keeler left Richmond and was named the principal at Armada Public Schools. He and his wife were also very active members of the Methodist Episcopal Church, where he was an officer and a leader of the choir and superintendent of the Sunday school. As Keeler lived out his remaining years in northern Macomb County, he was surrounded by his six children, who all stayed in the area, and his many grandchildren.

Dubbed the "Grand Old Man of Macomb," Keeler died due to heart failure at the age of eighty-two in October 1908. It seemed his time as a soldier in the Civil War followed him to the grave. It so happened that Keeler had served at the Battle of Chattanooga with a much younger soldier named Daniel Johnson, who not only fought alongside him but also served time with him as a prisoner of war in 1863. Well, news soon arrived from Pontiac, Michigan, that Johnson had dropped dead at the age of sixty-two on the very same day that his former commanding officer met his demise. Just four weeks earlier, the two veterans had been honored at a gathering for the ex-prisoners of the Twenty-Second Infantry. Old friends of Keeler described him as a noble character and one of the bravest and best soldiers who ever lived.

JOE LOUIS

Boxer Turned Horse Enthusiast

While heavyweight boxing champion Joe Louis was known for his talents with his meaty fists in the ring, he also had a lighter side. He loved horses: breeding them, riding and training them and then showing them off at exclusive events. In 1938, this unusual hobby led Louis to Shelby Township, where he purchased five hundred acres at Spring Hill Farms for $100,000.

To appreciate the uniqueness of a world-famous boxer landing in Macomb County, one must take a look back at his history. Born in Alabama in 1914, Louis, whose given name was Joseph Barron, moved to Detroit as a child, and his mother, hoping to keep him out of trouble, insisted he take violin lessons. Joe had other plans, using the money for lessons at the local recreation center, where he was taught to box. Once he began fighting in the ring, he changed his name to Joe Louis so his mother wouldn't catch on to what he was up to. He started his amateur career when he was twenty years old and took his share of knock downs before rising up to become

Joe Louis at Spring Hills Farms in Shelby Township. *Library of Congress.*

the hardest hitter the sport had yet to see. He went on to reign as the world heavyweight boxing champion from 1937 to 1949, with a brief hiatus from wearing the gloves professionally, when he joined the army in 1942. Still, he didn't stray far from the ring, participating in ninety-six bouts, including many charity exhibitions, earning donations for the Army Fund and Navy Reserve. In the U.S. Army, Louis attained the rank of sergeant and also the love of the people for his good nature.

A story in a local paper in 1946 after Louis defeated two opponents noted that experts felt he wasn't as good as he'd been before serving in the military, but if some contenders didn't materialize, he would remain the champion forever.

The land in Shelby Township that Louis decided to invest in also has its own remarkable history. Originally called Spring Hill Farm, the property was owned by Peter Lerich, and the farmhouse was marked by a massive cedar known as the "Beacon Tree." In the pre–Civil War era, Lerich was a conductor on the Underground Railroad, and he and some neighbors dug a huge hole, deep enough to hold several people, and hauled the tree in place on top of it. Runaway slaves arrived at the tree, walked along a fence line and slid down a pole, where they were hidden underground from slave catchers while receiving food and shelter from the Lerich family. Moving only at night, they would soon resume their journey north to Canada and freedom.

After Louis purchased the farm, a story came about with roots that traveled right back to the Lerich family. In a 1940 column sports columnist for the *New York Journal* Bill Corum praised the modest prize fighter. It seems as a new property owner, Louis was riding a horse and surveying his land when he came across a rickety old wooden shanty with smoke coming from the chimney. Stopping at the site, Louis observed an elderly couple coming out of the shack and asked them if it was their home. When they replied it was, he asked, "Doesn't it get pretty cold at night?" The couple told him indeed it did, but it was the only home the farm had now and they hoped the new owner wouldn't make them leave. Louis quickly told them there was no chance of that and invited them to move to the main house up the hill, telling them it would be warm and dry and they could get other things they might need. A good deed, but the story didn't end there. It turned out the older man in the squatter's cabin was Peter Lerich's grandson Wig Lerich and his wife. The tenant house they were moving into had been built by their own grandfather one hundred years before.

As Louis took possession of the large property, he had lots of plans. He utilized some of the space as a personal training camp. Spring Hill Farm was turned into a riding stable, with the toolshed and cattle barn converted into horse stables. He then added a track, bleachers and box seats so horse enthusiasts could enjoy shows on the property. The house was renovated and converted into a well-known restaurant and nightclub for Louis's friends and area residents. Lots of advertisements, including in newspapers and on signs, invited everyone to come out Springhill Farms on Hamlin Road to enjoy southern fried chicken, steak, porkchops, seafood, beer, wine, liquor and horseback riding. A blurb in a local newspaper right after Louis purchased the property said he had been advised by friends to purchase a gun for protection, but once he moved to the house in Shelby Township, he decided the weapon wasn't necessary and turned it over to the Macomb County Sheriff's Department.

Regular attention was given to Louis's investment in Shelby Township over the next few years. News outlets reported that in January 1941, the main house on the farm burned down and the loss was estimated at $3,000. In September of that same year a headline in the *Port Huron Times Herald* read, "Negro Killed at Roadhouse," referring to Spring Hill Farms, where a thirty-two-year-old man died after being hit over the head with a chair during a fight on the premises. Deputy sheriffs were called to the scene at 1:00 a.m. after shots were fired inside the building. Some six hundred members of the Ford Progressive Club were holding a dance at the roadhouse when newcomers objected to the thirty-five-cent cover charge. A month later, in October 1941, an exclusive horse show was hosted at the farm, with top-ranking fillies from the best stables in the Midwest competing for honors.

The competition was to include classes for three- and five-gaited horses, harness horses, ponies and jumpers. Louis planned to attend the event, likely his last public appearance before going into the army. Spring Hill Farms continued to operate successfully for several more years, hosting several charitable events before Louis's financial issues required the sale of the property in 1944. The Conservation Department in Michigan bought 428 acres, with plans to add parking, sanitary facilities, picnic and playground areas, which became part of the Utica-Rochester Recreation Area.

Louis struggled financially for the remainder of his life. He was married four times and had six children and tried to launch a food franchise business in the 1960s, served as a greeter at Caesar's Palace in Las Vegas and battled an addiction to cocaine. Heart trouble had him a wheelchair for the last few years of his life, and he died in April 1981 at the age of sixty-six.

JoAnn Burgess

A True Friend and Lifelong Educator

A stickler for perfection, when JoAnn Burgess made up her mind to do something, she gave it 100 percent. It was evident in her classrooms as an elementary school teacher for decades and in retirement when she ran Shelby Township's Burgess-Shadbush Nature Center, named in her honor.

Burgess was born in Detroit in 1934 to Truman and Ruth Burgess and grew up in the city along with her sister, Shirley. Their father, Truman, owned the Utica Pharmacy for many years. Burgess graduated from Denby High School before heading off to Stephens College, an all-girls school in Missouri, to pursue a teaching degree. Upon graduation in 1957, she returned to Michigan and moved into her parents' new home just off 24 Mile Road in Shelby Township. Shortly thereafter, she began her teaching career at Utica Community Schools and remained there for forty-two years. Her niece and nephew Robert and Ruth Peters said Burgess was extremely driven and earned a master's degree in education from the University of Michigan and later a degree from Michigan State that certified her as an outdoor educator. In fact, it seemed that for much of her life, she never stopped going, sometimes working around the clock on projects for her students or her volunteer groups.

A much beloved teacher, Burgess initially taught a variety of subjects but soon settled on music and environmental science. Playing the piano, the

JoAnn Burgess. *Courtesy of the Burgess family.*

flute, the violin and the organ were all in Burgess's repertoire. She also organized the Morgan Elementary School talent show for many years and was the first one on the floor teaching the younger students how to square dance. A Girl Scout leader in Shelby Township for decades, at one point, Burgess had logged camping trips with her scouts to all fifty states. In an interview published in a local newspaper in 2007, Burgess said she always felt teaching was more than a job, it was a profession that brought a lot satisfaction to the person involved in it. She retired in 1999 and devoted nearly all of her time to working with the Shelby Township Parks and Recreation Department, specifically its director, David Moore, to provide a place and a schedule of programs so residents could learn about the area's history and nature.

Once a location was secured at a log cabin at Riverbends Park, Burgess took over planning and managing programs. Jim Gammicchia, coordinator of Nature Center at Riverbends Park, said Burgess literally did a little bit of everything, from registering people for programs to answering phones and showing patrons around the center. She hosted nature tales and pioneer programs and was particularly fond of hosting special holiday events. He said Burgess was very creative, making all the crafts for the program and really served as her own Pinterest, coming up with new ideas all the time. She kept things very organized at the center and was big on keeping things in bins. She loved hosting camps for kids, including a very popular archery program. The nature center quickly grew into a major focal point in the township. In addition to a variety of interesting programs, the center itself has all kinds of critters to visit, including snakes, fish, rabbits, turtles and the occasional spider. Many of the animals come to the center because they require special attention due to illness or injury, and they are nursed back to health by the staff. In fact, Burgess's enthusiasm for all things related to nature was infectious. When she launched what is now an annual program at the nature center called The *Night the Animals Talk*, in no time, Bob Peters donned a skunk costume, learned lines Burgess had written for his character and found himself standing along trails outside the center ready to entertain the children. A particularly interesting and amusing lesson Burgess shared

JoAnn Burgess helps children at the Burgess-Shadbush Nature Center, named in her honor. *Courtesy of the Burgess-Shadbush Nature Center.*

with children at the nature center was centered on the origins of the phrase "sleep tight don't let the bedbugs bite" and how it related to settlers from the 1800s. It was shared during an interview Burgess did with a local newspaper:

Pointing at a mattress on a bed inside a log cabin, Burgess said, "Lift that up. See? No box spring, just rope. Well, people would have to tighten those ropes to secure the mattress, which prompted the term sleep tight. The mattresses were filled with hay, which often attracted bugs, so was born the don't let the bed bugs bite term. A normal good night to settlers' children became sleep tight don't let the bed bugs bite."

The Burgess-Shadbush Nature Center was renamed in 2005 to honor Burgess. It is open five days a week, and she spent much of her "retirement" working there. Obviously touched to see the local nature center named in her honor, Burgess didn't sit well in the spotlight, not fond of the accolades and attention, she always just wanted to get on with sharing her love of the outdoors with the kids. Still, she commented at the time that it was an honor she never expected and was duly impressed that people thought she was worthy of such attention, especially for something she loved so much.

Her passions beyond the nature center were books and shopping. She also enjoyed spending time with her two schnauzers, Ozzie and Harriet, gardening and doing needlepoint, on the rare occasion that she was actually sitting down. The Peters, who eventually moved into Burgess's family home to take care of her, said she liked to try everything but wasn't always successful at the tasks. They both had a good laugh recalling the time she insisted on mowing the front lawn on a riding mower and quickly hit a large cement ornamental deer that her father had placed in the yard years ago. The damage to the deer was minimal, but Burgess never offered to cut the lawn again, deciding she'd stick to what she knew she was good at, which didn't include driving. She did create a huge garden with a dozen bird feeders that brought feathered friends to the family's two-acre parcel year-round. When Bob Peters crafted a bird feeder out a miniature beer keg, Burgess wasn't satisfied with just one for her yard. Soon she had half a dozen of them packed with seeds for the birds who visited often.

Bob Peters said Burgess loved her life and loved doing just about everything you can think of and in particular couldn't wait for the Christmas season to roll around. She was like a big kid, filled with mischief and excitement. JoAnn Burgess passed away in June 2018 at the age of eighty-four. Local mayor Jacqueline Noonan called Burgess a wonderful teacher, naturalist, activist, friend and someone who contributed something special to so many lives in so many ways. Noonan also remembered her friend as a member of the Utica Heritage Association for forty years, hugely responsible for publishing a history of Utica and for taking part in numerous cemetery walks at the Utica Cemetery over four decades.

10

St. Clair Shores

A tight-knit community from the start, the city was first incorporated as the Village of St. Clair Shores in 1925 and was a part of Erin Township. The eastern portion of the township occupied by St. Clair Shores was partitioned from Erin Township to become Lake Township. The Village of St. Clair Shores would remain a part of Lake Township and was recognized as the largest village in the United States until the city was incorporated in 1951. Its location on the shores of Lake Saint Clair had the city growing from a resort community to a suburban city rapidly after World War II. The city was once home to an amusement park named Jefferson Beach that featured the longest roller coaster in the United States. It's also known for its Nautical Mile—a strip of Jefferson Avenue between Nine Mile and Ten Mile Roads featuring many retail establishments, bars, restaurants and marinas. Today, the city's population exceeds fifty-nine thousand in just over fourteen miles.

TOM WELSH

A Youthful, Colorful, Eager Politician

He campaigned on his youth and ability to make things happen in the city and the idea carried twenty-one-year-old Thomas Stanton Welsh II to his first elected post on the St. Clair Shores Village Council in 1947. A

Democrat, he served several terms on the village council, and then when St. Clair Shores became a city, he was elected a councilman again, getting the highest number of votes among even seasoned candidates. The council bypassed him that first year for the mayor's seat, but the next year, 1953, it appointed him to the top spot. A new city charter amendment in 1955 said voters would pick the mayor going forward, and Welsh was on the ballot, winning in a four-to-one landslide against his opponents—a huge accomplishment for such a young man.

Welsh was born in St. Clair Shores in 1926 to Stanton Thomas Welsh and Delphine Delisle Welsh, and he was actually following in his father's footsteps. Stanton Welsh had served as a constable and justice of the peace in Lake Township and was a state representative from Macomb County in 1939–40. The elder Welsh died at just forty-three years old in 1943. Tom Welsh said his father's death led him to leave high school after finishing the tenth grade because somebody had to go out and work. He started a cartage company. The business grew into Welsh Moving and Storage. He bought two more trucks, and his wife, Fern, became one of his drivers.

Welsh, who had been the city's mayor for several terms now, utilized his aggressive manner to spearhead unprecedented growth in the city in the 1950s. In 1950, St. Clair Shores had a population of 19,800, and in just four years' time, residency jumped to 37,000. The city issued $5 million in building permits, including homes and apartments. All that growth was in just twelve square miles, many of the homes being built off East Jefferson Avenue along the canal frontage leading to Lake St. Clair. Welsh said the reason for the boom was the recent completion of a $600,000 sanitary sewer extension from 10 Mile to the city limits at East 14 Mile Road.

While the young politician tackled massive growth in his city, things became challenging, but he had no problem standing up to anyone or anything that might halt his city's progress. He put a real wrinkle in the state highway department's plan to run the I-94 expressway right down Harper Avenue, virtually splitting St. Clair Shores in half, driving out business and burying the city. Welsh fought against the plan for nearly five years before the highway department re-routed I-94 to follow the border between St. Clair Shores and Eastpointe and Roseville.

As he was enjoying his first decade in politics, Walsh had gone into real estate and was making $15,000 a year. He and his wife and three young children lived in a bungalow on Lake St. Clair. Standing six feet, one inch tall, weighing over 300 pounds and filling out a size 54 suit, Welsh was an impressive and somewhat intimidating man. He remained at the ready

St. Clair Shores mayor Tom Welsh giving a speech at the Women's Civic League in 1954. *St. Clair Shores Historical Commission Photograph Collection.*

when the negative headlines with claims of illegal dealings started rolling in. When several complaints were made against Welsh, a Macomb County one-man jury in the form of Circuit Court Judge Timothy Quinn of Caro charged that Welsh deliberately confused his roles as mayor and real estate broker to enrich himself with $21,575. Quinn sought Welsh's removal from office and sent an eighteen-page petition to Governor G. Mennen Williams seeking a decision on the issue. When Welsh refused to testify at a hearing on the matter, he was charged with contempt of court and sent to the Macomb County Jail.

The thirty-one-year-old mayor made headlines in January 1957 when he was found mopping the floors on his third day in the slammer. Having been sentenced to sixty days, Welsh was a little shaken at becoming at inmate and admitted he was lonesome for his wife and three children, noting that he'd never spent a night away from his wife since they were married. He was also adamant that he would stay in jail for as long as it took because that's what was right, as someone was trying to smear him politically.

Ironically, Welsh, a member of the board of county supervisors, had a hand in seeing the modern jail built in 1955, so at least he was being housed in relative luxury, with indoor plumbing. He was released on bond on the fourth day of his stay. In April that year, despite the allegations and charges, he was elected to his fifth term as mayor.

Still, the issue dragged on throughout the year, and in October, three hundred people crowded a city council meeting to pledge their support for the mayor, holding signs that read "Thank you Tom" and "We Will Do Our Own Ousting." Welsh told his supporters that was just the kind of blood transfusion he needed, and he would have all the blood drained from his body before he'd resign his position. Later, the crowd broke into cheers when the council passed a resolution that expressed its confidence in the integrity of Welsh and the desire to have him continue to serve in the office to which he was elected. As 1957, came to a close, it looked like the issue might be resolved, but the 355-pound mayor was hospitalized on the day he was due in court, possibly having suffered a heart attack. After a brief hospitalization, it was concluded that Welsh didn't have a heart attack. In January 1959, Governor Williams found no reason to act on misconduct charges, and Welsh ran unopposed for his sixth two-year term as mayor of St. Clair Shores.

The popular mayor also grabbed headlines for more frivolous things. In 1954, a story was circulated across the state about how a water boy saved a blond woman in distress. It seems a young St. Clair Shores housewife was bleaching her hair and didn't realize the city was repairing a water main and shut the water off on her street. Welsh got a frantic call from the lady saying if the water didn't get turned back on pronto, she was going to be bald. Welsh dispatched a police officer to the scene with a five-gallon can of water, and he rinsed the lady's hair, much to her relief.

In 1960, Welsh, thirty-four, announced his candidacy for Macomb County drain commissioner and said economics played a role in his decision, as the part-time mayoral post paid $1,800 a year while the drain commissioner salary was $12,000 annually. Still a controversial character when he ran for drain commissioner in November 1960, Welsh defeated his challenger and launched a thirty-two-year career as the public works commissioner—the job title was changed along the way. He oversaw the development of sewers and drains during much growth in Macomb County, and when he stepped down from the post in 1992, he still held a seat on the county road commission. He was also instrumental in the development of the regional parks system as a member of the Huron-Clinton Metropolitan Authority.

Dedication of the Chapaton Pump Station, Congressman James G. O'Hara is speaking. Tom Welsh, former St. Clair Shores mayor and Intracounty Drainage Board chair, is to the left of the congressman. In the background between Welsh and O'Hara is Vice President Hubert Humphrey. *St. Clair Shores Historical Commission Photograph Collection.*

You could say he retired to Richmond, where he owned several different parcels of land, but he was always working on some business deal. He passed away in 2000 at the age of seventy-three after suffering a heart attack. He left a legacy to be envied according to Walter Mathes, who worked for Welsh for twenty years:

> *He was Mr. Democrat in Macomb County. He was a very powerful man. He knew everybody in the county, and he was the first to know what was going on.*

MARGARET ROETS

Historian with a Flemish Flare

When you work to preserve history, be it your family's or for the community, it's usually a labor of love. It certainly was for longtime St. Clair Shores resident Margaret Pattyn Roets. In fact, when friends nominated her for a county award for all her hard work as a historian, they had to trick her into going to the awards ceremony. In 2010, Roets was honored with the Alexander Macomb Award from the Macomb County Historical Commission, the first resident of the city to be given the honor. Modest and not one to bask in any glory, the eighty-nine-year-old Roets's hard work was recognized by over one thousand people at a local park.

In 1921, Margaret Pattyn Roets was born in Detroit to Evarist and Marie (Vandewalle) Pattyn, who had emigrated from Belgium in 1920. She had two brothers: Edward, born in 1923, followed by Albert in 1924. She recalled her parents as extremely hardworking and very eager to learn English and become citizens of the United States, which they did as soon as the law would allow it. Marie Pattyn was also very frugal, an admirable trait that helped the family get through the Depression and the years afterward. Roets said she actually never realized how really poor her family was simply because everyone they knew faced the same predicament, so it didn't really matter. Family life was simple then, as visiting friends and family was the highlight of the week. There were no such things as babysitters—if the parents went out, so did the children. If the little ones grew tired, a simple pillow was tossed in a corner of the room and they would curl up and nap until it was time to go home.

Family entertainment consisted of card playing or building puzzles around the dining room table or, if there was a spare dime, going to the Mack Theater on Mack Avenue for a Saturday matinee. Cowboy movies with Tom Mix and Buck Rogers was the standard fare, but there were also short films called *The Chapters*, thrillers with cliffhangers to entice moviegoers to return week after week. Summer days were spent at Chandler Park, where all the cousins would meet up to go swimming in a baby pool that was only two feet deep.

In 1949, Margaret Pattyn married Albert Roets, they had no children. She was employed in the finance department at Park Davis & Co., later known as Warner Lambert, for forty-one years. When she retired in 1982, she started volunteering with the St. Clair Shores historical community, as she and her husband had moved to the city in 1955, when they were the last ones on their street to build a home in the then up-and-coming neighborhood. Upon retiring, Roets not only became involved in the Historical Society of St. Clair Shores, serving as both a trustee and later the president, but she was also involved in the history of her Belgian heritage. An active member in the Flemish American Association and Genealogical Society of Flemish Americans in Southeast Michigan, she documented and researched their heritage. The publication *Gazette van Detroit,* also benefited from Roets's volunteer time; she served as a proofreader and handled the finances. In addition to volunteering for many organizations, Roets put herself front and center for special speaking engagements for local nonprofits and historical groups, giving presentations on everything from Christmas traditions in Belgium to tips on how to do your own family genealogy research.

Roets's longtime friends Rich and Mary Jacobs nominated her for the prestigious county award. In a nomination application, they said she was an amazing president for the Historical Society of St. Clair Shores, serving in that position for nearly ten years. Always holding the city's best interest at heart, Roets was described as a kind, wonderful person with a great heart, an easygoing manner and an ability to work well with people sharing her deep passion for history. In St. Clair Shores specifically, the Jacobses listed her work volunteering at the Selinsky-Green Farmhouse Museum, including activities like teas, holiday events and programing. There was also a Wednesday Working Group that welcomed Roets's attention. Members spent afternoons crafting items to sell in the museum gift shop and working

St. Clair Shores historian Margaret Pattyn Roets accepts the Alexander Macomb Award from Macomb County Historical Commission member Suzanne Pixley (*left*). *From the Macomb Daily.*

on beautiful, hand-crafted quilts that were raffled off at the St. Clair Shores Art Fair each year.

In a newspaper story from the year of the award presentation, Mary Jacobs described how she had to practically demand that Roets take a ride with her on the night of the awards presentations at Veterans Park in St. Clair Shores. A regular music series was going on at the park, and Jacobs didn't say where they were going. Roets reportedly proclaimed she was pleased, honored and surprised when her name was called to come to the stage for the honor. She also modestly admitted being involved in a number of activities in her community related to history. Eastpointe mayor Suzanne Pixley, a member of the Macomb County Historical Commission and friend of Roets, presented her with the award. Pixley noted that Roets had gone above and beyond to preserve the city's history; in fact, one would be hard-pressed to find her at home because she was always out and about working on something.

Margaret celebrated her ninety-ninth birthday on May 9, 2020, and in the middle of a pandemic, dozens of friends hosted a drive-by party complete with honking horns and colorful signs. She sat curbside with a face mask in place, likely slightly embarrassed at what all the fuss was about.

11

Sterling Heights

The city of Sterling Heights has a rich and interesting history that goes back nearly two hundred years to when settlers called it Jefferson Township. Lewis Drake, born in New York and a direct descendant of famed sixteenth-century navigator Sir Francis Drake, came to the area near Dodge Park and Utica Roads in 1832. He shelled out eighteen shillings (less than four dollars) an acre for his farm, and by 1835, the area had become known as Jefferson Township. By 1880, it had become Sterling Township, a prosperous area of farms with a population of 2,088. It was incorporated as Sterling Heights in 1968. Now the fourth-largest city in the state with a population exceeding 132,000, Sterling Heights is located 19 miles north of downtown Detroit and covers some 36.7 square miles.

CHIEF MAURICE FOLTZ

Launching a Police Force

When Kit DiMambro reflects on her father's life, she knows he was well respected and accomplished, but the main word she thinks of is integrity. She stated that Chief Maurice Foltz had the most upright character of anyone she's ever known and probably will ever meet. She could bring home a C on her report card and he wouldn't be pleased, but there was no punishment. In contrast, if you told a lie or were sneaky or did anything that showed a lack of integrity, he wanted a reason why. DiMambro said her goal in life is to be like him.

Foltz was born in 1927 to Orville and Golden Foltz in Romeo and grew up in the village of Romeo, graduating from high school when he was sixteen. He joined the Romeo Volunteer Fire Department when he was eighteen and helped get a rescue squad in place. By 1956, he had become interested in police work as well and joined the Oak Park public safety department, which included both police and fire. He attained the rank of sergeant there but, after seven years, was recruited to be chief in Royal Oak and then Farmington Hills before going to Sterling Township to start a department from the ground up.

It was 1966, and Sterling Township was a community of 22,000 with no police force when Foltz was hired to create one. In an oral history interview recorded through a project at Sterling Heights Library, he took on the chief's role for $9,000 a year and had twelve officers and four cadets. They were housed in a room at the city offices that included four chairs, a card table, a phone and a phonebook. This small crew was responsible for covering 36.8 square miles; it was a struggle, but they did it. Foltz likened the experience to a fisherman owning a big lake. It had never been fished in, so it didn't matter where you threw the line, you always had something on the other end of the hook. Being the new "fish" in this large city pond meant many people, used to not having police coverage, simply wanted to test the new regime. It might be someone racing along the expressway thinking he could outrun such a sparse force or thinking participating in any illegal activity was no problem with so few officers around. The city's population soared over the next two decades to 100,000.

In twenty-five years of police work, Foltz had every case imaginable. Self-proclaimed State Nazi leader Russell Roberts, sixty-four, faced libel charges in Farmington Hills in 1965 while Foltz was the chief of police in that community. He was a great follower of George Lincoln Rockwell, the man who launched the American Nazi Party in 1959. The charges stemmed from Roberts trying to induce a fourteen-year-old boy to spread leaflets that libeled Black people. Described as a man with a paunch and frizzled mustache, Roberts was charged with a misdemeanor and told the judge that he believed in Adolf Hitler 1,000 percent. Foltz said he especially resented Roberts's actions because of how it might influence a fourteen-year-old kid and teach him to hate.

In 1967, as chief in Sterling Township, Foltz handled a pair of investigations related to lunch bucket bombs found in the girls' restroom at Shelby Junior

High School. The device was found before students arrived at school that morning and was the second one in as many weeks that was set up but didn't explode. Foltz said it appeared the person who was placing the harmless bombs was simply seeking recognition. The person placing the devices had entered the building after moving some plywood that was covering a broken window. The bomb was enclosed in a gray metal lunch pail, and Foltz took it into a nearby field and opened it. The bucket contained a metal pipe held in place by wires and an alarm clock filled with gravel and kerosene. The culprit was never found.

In 1975, Foltz found himself in charge of convicted burglar turned FBI informant John J. Whalen, thirty, who was residing in Macomb County. He was the government's star witness for the perjury and bribery trial of Michigan Supreme Court justice John Swainson. Testifying against Swainson, a former Michigan governor, Whelan helped ensure the judge was found guilty of perjury, although he was acquitted on the bribery charge. Whelan claimed he had arranged for a $20,000 bribe for Swainson to influence other high justices to order a new trial for him on his burglary convictions. When he brought these accusations to the attention of the FBI in 1972, Whalen even carried a concealed microphone while meeting with Harvey Wish, a bail bondsman who was alleged to have acted as the go between for Whalen with Swainson. In return for his testimony, John Whalen was promised he could serve his time in a federal prison under an assumed name in exchange for his cooperation. Four days after the judge was convicted, Whalen's St. Clair Shores home went up in flames. A week later, when Whalen failed to turn himself into authorities at the Sterling Heights Police Department to begin his sentence out of state, he was kidnapped and tortured by men he refused to identify. When he turned up at the police station a day later, he was suffering from two gunshot wounds and thirty-four cigarette burns over much of his body. It was implied that this turn of events could have been related to another informant lead Whalen provided that led to the arrest of a dozen people who fenced $4.5 million in merchandise annually. He was hospitalized under heavy guard, and his attorney claimed he was absolutely in terror and fear for his family's life. It wasn't clear if Whalen would be expected to serve his prison sentence after he recovered, but it turned out he was sent to jail and later lost his appeal of his initial burglary conviction.

DeMombro described her father, Chief Foltz, as a true cop, always on 24/7, even if it meant getting out his bed in the middle of the night to go on a call. She and her three sisters grew up in Sterling Heights admiring

Sterling Heights police chief Maurice Foltz at the dedication of the city's Justice Center that bears his name. *Courtesy of the Foltz family.*

his steadfastness and impeccable character. He embraced integrity after work too, and if someone tried to buy him a drink when he was out to dinner with his family, he declined it.

When Foltz retired in 1981, he was operating a department that included a budget of $8 million. The first budget he set up, hastily written on a legal pad, amounted to $74,000 for the year for everything. Foltz agreed the department had definitely come a long way under his leadership. He didn't rest in retirement though; his wife, Marjorie, had owned a dress shop in Romeo for many years and he purchased that building and several others to create what became known as Romeo Frontier Town. A popular local shopping attraction for families, he refurbished all the buildings himself with an Old West motif. The idea came from an image he noticed on the back of a cereal box on the table while his young daughters were having breakfast. He told them he was going to create that town, and a few years later, he did.

Chief Foltz passed away in 2008 at the age of eighty. He was survived by his wife of fifty-six years, Marjorie, four children, twelve grandchildren and nine great-grandchildren.

MAYOR RICHARD NOTTE

Regular Guy in a Fancy Hat

If you were going to imagine what a suburban politician might be like in the mid-1980s, a smooth-talking man wearing a suit and tie would likely come to mind. Yet for nearly thirty years in Sterling Heights, the top guy wore opened-collared shirts, a big grin and his signature hat, a black fedora.

Richard Notte was simply an average working man, employed as a welder and union representative at Ford Motor Company, a husband, father of six and someone interested in making a real difference in his community. When he decided to seek a seat on the Sterling Heights City Council in 1985, he likely didn't realize he'd be serving nearly thirty years at the council table, the majority as mayor of the city. Sterling Heights has a city manager form of government, with the mayor simply a figurehead for the city, but you couldn't stop Notte. He jumped right into things from the start and attended nearly every event hosted in the city, be it a car wash, school concert or chamber of commerce meeting.

In 1993, Notte moved from a councilman's chair to the mayor's office, the first mayor not appointed by a majority of the city council but instead elected by popular vote of the people. He defeated Mayor Steve Rice in a hard-fought battle—the main issue was strip malls. Rice wanted to stop

Mayor Richard Notte in his trademark fedora. *From the Macomb Daily.*

allowing them in the city, noting many empty storefronts, but Notte said he wanted to be fair to developers who had already invested in the city and vowed to help keep and fill the stores already in place. He went on to serve eleven two-year terms in the mayor's office and was beloved by a wide majority of voters in the city. He was a major advocate for jobs, the union and business, literally attending thousands of ribbon cuttings during his tenure.

Having Notte give all that attention to so many things paid off big for the city in 2009. It was announced that the Chrysler Assembly Plant was going to close down within eighteen months, with a loss of 1,200 jobs and untold revenue to the city. Notte went at the problem full bore, rallying unions, residents and officials across the county and state to help him save the plant. His tenacity paid off. By the end of 2010, Chrysler had announced the plant would remain open, saving those 1,200 jobs, and it was going to invest millions of dollars in a new, more efficient painting facility that promised more jobs.

Going to bat for people wasn't anything new for Notte. Macomb County executive Mark Hackel learned that quickly in 2000 when he was a captain with the Macomb County Sheriff's Department and considering a run for sheriff. Notte asked Hackel to meet him for lunch one day. Hackel wasn't sure if the mayor was looking to talk him out of running for sheriff but was pleasantly surprised to have Notte not only agree to endorse him but also rally everyone he knew to do the same. When Hackel won the election for sheriff, it was Notte who planned his victory party at a local UAW Hall.

Many felt the best thing about Notte was simply, well, Notte: he was authentic, meant what he said and was a willing listener and dependable problem solver. One evening, he was being yelled and screamed at during the public comments portion of a city council meeting, and when the man

Macomb County executive Mark Hackel shares a laugh with Mayor Richard Notte at a meeting in Mount Clemens. *From the* Oakland Press.

was done, Notte said, in an even keel, "So I guess you won't be asking for one of my lawn signs?" It was light and broke up the tension of the meeting, and then Notte addressed what the complainant had to say.

Notte, of course, faced endless ups and downs helping to manage a city whose population was growing and changing all the time. A couple of big stories that garnered plenty of attention for the city actually involved the longtime city manager Steve Duchane. A nineteen-month newspaper strike with the *Detroit News* and *Detroit Free Press* in the mid-1990s had the city's police department responding to major issues along the strike lines at the Sterling Heights Plan at 16 Mile and Mound Road. Incidents of vandalism and violence prompted major overtime pay for police officers and cost the city nearly $1 million. Notte and a majority of the city council backed a decision to force City Manager Steve Duchane to resign his position, making him take the fall for accepting $600,000 from the Detroit Newspaper Agency to offset costs the city incurred during the strike. After Duchane resigned, angry voters cleaned house at the council table that November, and he was rehired with Notte's blessing. The mayor said he'd had a change of attitude about the issue and would work with Duchane. Unfortunately, a Duchane problem arose in the city again in 2003 when an anonymous letter revealed that the city manager, who had been in place since 1987, lied about his educational background and did not have a college degree. The city council, backed by Notte, fired Duchane, although he seemed to land on his feet, leaving with a severance package that exceeded $100,000.

Even with the bumps in the road, Hackel said Notte adored being the mayor, and if he could have been mayor of the county, he'd have jumped right in. He went beyond Sterling Heights, going to fairs, festivals and dinners across the area to show his support for others. He made friends wherever he'd go, and when he visited other union plants, workers quickly recognized him and wanted to shake his hand.

Family was also important to Notte, even though with his job and work for the city, he was spread pretty thin. In June 2001, Notte suffered a personal tragedy when his nineteen-year-old daughter, Andrea Notte, died after her Ford Explorer was hit by a train in Clinton Township. The Clinton Township police determined that the driver was at fault; witnesses stated she ignored lights and whistles from the train, which was traveling at thirty-eight miles per hour when the crash occurred. In the days after the incident, county officials said the site was part of a three-year plan to install twenty-four crossing gates at intersections and one would be in place there within weeks.

Sterling Heights mayor Richard Notte speaks at a meeting of local officials in Mount Clemens. *From the* Oakland Press.

The loss of his wife Margaret, fifty-seven, in 2004 after a cancer battle was another devasting blow for the mayor. The losses set him back for a time, but his city still had a hold on his heart.

In 2009, the Southeast Michigan Council of Governments awarded Notte its Regional Ambassador Award, and in 2011, colleagues and peers across the state presented Notte with the Michigan Municipal League's prestigious Michael A. Guido Leadership and Public Service Award. Two years later, he was inducted into the Macomb Hall of Fame and was recognized for his contributions to improving the economic, family and community life of Macomb County. During his induction into the Macomb Hall of Fame in 2013, he said he didn't really like being called a politician; he'd rather be called a representative, because that's what he did, worked for the people.

Notte retired in 2004 following forty-five years with Ford Motor Company, where he was a welder, and held several elected positions with the UAW. He finally had to take a break from his beloved city in August 2014 to battle pancreatic cancer. He lost the fight just two months later. Notte was hailed as the people's man, whose concern for what was going on in the city was unmatched. His son Michael perhaps said it best during a eulogy to his father.

Recalling his father's first campaign for office and the literature he printed that read, "Tie a knot for Notte," Michael said the gesture was exceedingly appropriate simply because his father was always about bringing people together.

MARJORIE UPTON DEFRANCIS

Saving Grandpa's House

The Upton House is listed in the National Register of Historical Places, and nothing pleased Marjorie Upton DeFrancis more than seeing her family's old homestead saved and restored. DeFrancis was the great-granddaughter of William and Sarah Upton, and their story began in Sterling Township in 1845.

William Upton, born in Leicestershire, England, moved to Sterling Township in 1845 when he was just ten years old. In 1861, William married seventeen-year-old Sarah Jeannette Aldrich, and according to research completed for the state historic marker, William and Sarah Aldrich Upton built the large two-story brick Victorian home in 1866 on 136 acres of land. They raised four children while living in the Upton House including Charles, Frank, Rena and Victor. In addition to farming, William sold fish caught in the Clinton River, and historic records reflect that William Upton and his brothers were active in the community, serving as road supervisors and even justices of the peace. In the 1870s, he became a real estate broker and owned the Upton Block, a three-story building on the northeast corner of Cass and Auburn Streets in Utica, where he sold dry goods, notions and gents' furnishings.

The Uptons owned the home until 1891, and then William Upton moved to Rochester, Michigan, where he spent the rest of his life. He and Sarah are buried in the Utica Cemetery. The home changed hands over the years, with the Heldt and Ahrens families residing there into the twentieth century. It was a boardinghouse in the mid-1900s and then an office building in 1960 and the city's parks and recreation offices in the 1970s. Even if there were a number of different owners of the old house at Dodge Park and Utica Roads, it was always the family home to Marjorie DeFrancis. She said her mother always pointed it out as the place where her grandfather, Frank, lived as a young boy.

Marjorie Upton Sayer was born on August 2, 1917, in Washington, Michigan, to Oren V. Sayre and Sarah Jeanette Upton Sayre. She had one sibling, a younger sister, Jeanette. She married Robert DeFrancis and had two children of her own, James and Roberta. During a sit-down interview in 1986 through an oral history project with the Sterling Heights Library, DeFrancis shared some of those early memories surrounding the Upton family. She recalled her great-grandfather William Upton as a big man with

William Upton and his wife, Sarah Aldrich Upton, and their granddaughter Sarah Jeanette Upton, the daughter of their son Frank. Pictured left to right are Sarah Upton, an unidentified girl, granddaughter Sarah and William. *Sterling Heights Public Library Local History Collection.*

a lot of white hair. He always seemed stern, not the kind of grandpa that would pick you up in his lap or give hugs. She was only six years old when he died. As for her grandparents, she said her grandmother kind of ran the show because her grandfather became a recluse after her own mother, Sarah Jeanette Upton Sayre, died at just thirty-eight years old in 1931.

There was Upton property all over the area, a farm near Stony Creek, eight acres in Shelby Township, a tenement house and farm and DeFrancis

The Upton House in Sterling Heights. *Sterling Heights Public Library Local History Collection.*

never recalled her grandfather working a day in his life. She said a great-aunt once said that the family lived off the Upton property. If they needed some money, they would just sell another twenty acres. DeFrancis said when her grandparents passed away, she and her sister held the last twenty acres, and that's where Stony Creek is located now.

The old Upton homestead was still standing in Sterling Heights, and officials were wondering what to do with it, so DeFrancis and her son, James Upton DeFrancis, attended the first meeting on the topic in 1980. Once ideas about tearing the house down for a parking lot were ruled out, the city hired an architectural firm to do a feasibility study. A plan to save and restore the house was presented in late August that same year, and city officials agreed to do it. DeFrancis shared that when she left that meeting, although it was after 11:00 p.m., she drove by the site of the Upton House and cried, saying, "Grampa we saved it for you." Too young to have ever visited the house when it was in her family, DeFrancis said she had been inside once when the owners invited her and her husband in for dinner and it was a thrill to touch the woodwork and walk the floors where her ancestors had been. Over the next two years, a devoted committee of volunteers worked to get the word out about the need for funding to

Marjorie Upton DeFrancis.
Sterling Heights Public Library Local History Collection.

restore the house. DeFrancis said they had a speakers' bureau set up committee members who would go out and speak to various groups, talking about the house and working to save it. DeFrancis recalled that the exhibits organized were particularly interesting with Upton memorabilia. Old photographs had been blown up to display; there was a mannequin wearing an old-fashioned lace bonnet, plus a display with farm equipment, including old saws and pitchforks.

The renovation was completed in October 1982, and many Upton family members, along with city officials and members of the cultural and history commissions, gathered for a ribbon-cutting ceremony. DeFrancis, her children and grandchildren were there, and despite the fact that she never actually lived in Sterling Heights, DeFrancis made sure her family legacy there remained intact.

An unusually vibrant and involved volunteer, DeFrancis left her own hearty legacy as an active and admired member of the Mount Clemens community, working tirelessly for nonprofits and groups related to the arts. She completed her associate degree, graduating magna cum laude, at Macomb Community College at the age of seventy-three. She enjoyed reading, politics, genealogy and bridge, and when she passed away in 2016 at the age of 98, her obituary proudly pointed out the world had lost an extraordinary woman. Today, the 151-year-old Victorian-style Upton house remains open to the public. The lower floor of the home houses repurposed furniture and information about the city's past, and the upstairs is a small museum with memorabilia, including historic photographs.

12

Utica

*I*t's been two hundred years since Revolutionary War soldier Nathanial Squire built a log cabin near a pair of Indian trails and the flowing Clinton River, becoming the first resident of the tiny town of Utica.

Initially platted with the name Harlow, McDougalville and Hog's Hollow were also short-lived names for the area, the latter moniker because legend says a wild boar was killed in the middle of the downtown area. Utica became a village in 1829 after President James Madison signed the paperwork naming the village after a settlement in New York. In 1932, it officially became a city.

Today, covering just 1.74 miles, Utica has a population of just under five thousand and, as in the mid-1900s, boasts a bustling downtown. Auburn Road draws people to restaurants, bars and, as of 2016, a huge minor league baseball stadium, the United Shore Professional Baseball League, one of the most high-tech facilities in the nation.

DR. WILLIAM BROWNELL

Attack on Doctor Almost Ends Stellar Career

Country doctors may have been the norm in small towns in the mid-1800s, but when Dr. William Brownell arrived in Utica, he was definitely there to leave his mark.

The son of George and Clarissa Brownell, the doctor was born in Michigan in 1830. In 1852, after Brownell graduated from the University of Michigan Medical School, he traveled to the village of Utica, eager to set up his practice. He married Jane Elizabeth Scudder there in 1856, and they had three children: William Jr., Elizabeth and Kate.

Establishing himself as a conscientious citizen, Brownell was postmaster of Utica from 1854 to 1856 and served two terms in the state legislature. He was described as having a strong, conservative voice, not shy about letting his words be heard in the halls of Lansing. Described as a War Democrat, Brownell was someone who was not deterred from what he believed to be errors in judgment put forth by his political opponents. In fact, in order to prove his loyalty to the Northern cause, Brownell enlisted in the Second Michigan Cavalry in 1861 as an assistant surgeon. When he was discharged three years later, he held the rank of acting brigade surgeon.

Returning home to Utica, Brownell resumed his work at a country doctor and was described as being strong and steady in body but with a quiet demeanor, making him a man of few words as he went about his rounds.

It was on a warm July evening in 1872 when the doctor, upon returning to his home after a visit to a patient in the village, was met near his barn by a man wielding a revolver. As the local newspaper of the day reported, the man, identified later as Lewis C. Butler, twenty-one, from Troy in Oakland County, followed Brownell into the barn and asked the doctor to perform an abortion on a woman who accompanied him, stating she was his wife.

The *Detroit Free Press* continued,

> *The doctor politely but firmly refused to aid them in their design and endeavored to persuade him from making the attempt, pointing out the danger to her life, besides the committing of a dreadful crime.*

The man then threatened the doctor as he continued to refuse to perform the act, and Brownell demanded he leave the premises. Just then, Butler pointed his gun at the doctor. Almost as quickly, the doctor lunged forward and grabbed the gun before the assailant could fire. A desperate struggle ensued: the doctor forced him out of the barn and pushed the gunman some forty feet toward the house before the assailant wrestled the gun away and shot the doctor in the right thigh.

Realizing he was shot, Brownell quickly threw the suspect on the ground and held him there until some of the neighbors, after hearing the screams of the doctor's family, came to his aid. They carried the doctor into his home,

Dr. William Brownell.
Courtesy of the Utica Heritage Association.

where his injuries could be tended to. The wound was described as an ugly one, the ball having hit the bone and glanced off, making a ragged hole completely through his thigh.

It was also reported that the news of the assault traveled through the village like wildfire, and it was all the local police could do to keep the townspeople from lynching Butler. The residents actually procured a rope and were ready to do the deed when word got back to them that the doctor's wound was not fatal. They turned Butler over to the police.

Had the ball from the revolver passed higher up or hit the opposite side of the bone, it would have been fatal.

Brownell continued to serve his community beyond his profession serving sixteen years on the local school board, ten of those years as president, earning the title father of the public schools. He also continued his stellar career as a country doctor and so it came as quite a shock when he passed away in 1884 at the age of fifty-three. It was reported that he suffered from Bright's Disease, which involved inflammation related to the kidneys. Local papers reported on the great loss of such an esteemed citizen not only to the Village of Utica but also the state and even the nation. His influence remained in both state and national level affairs for years to come.

LIBRARIAN NAOMI GIBBING

An Encyclopedia of Local History

When the first members of Naomi Gibbing's family came to the village of Utica in 1830, it's hard to imagine that the tiny town, covering less than two miles, would welcome five generations over the next centuries.

Gibbing's great-great-grandfather was a county surveyor and Macomb County sheriff, and her great-grandfather Charles Adair was a city surveyor and postmaster. Born in the city in 1916 to Frank and Grace (Mott) Gibbing, Naomi was one of seven children. Her father was prominent in the community, serving as the city's water and sewer superintendent for many years. As a nod to his prestige, the Utica Historical Society archives has an engraved invitation Frank received in 1929 to attend the official opening of the Ambassador Bridge, which connects Michigan to Canada.

Gibbing's love for words and the books that contained them began at a young age. A local newspaper quotes her sister as stating their mother had to take books away from her and make her go out and get some fresh air. After graduating from Utica High School in 1934 as the salutatorian, she was described as a warm, soft-spoken person interested in preserving local history and serving her community as the librarian. She had a genuine rapport with both children and adults and was devoted to helping them find what they were looking for on her library shelves.

In fact, she was often referred to as "an encyclopedia of information"; it wasn't unusual to see patrons by passing the library card catalogues to instead defer to Gibbing.

Local historian Patricia Hallman said Gibbing was known for being friendly, studious, a chain smoker and always eager to share information about the municipality her family had called home for more than a century. Gibbing so enjoyed collecting "stuff" related to the subject, and in her later years, she began donating documents and letters to the historic archives now housed in the basement at the Utica Public Library.

In 1967, the Michigan State Board of Education granted Gibbing a Librarian's Permanent Professional Certificate; in 1969, a local elementary school was named Naomi Gibbing Elementary; and in 1981, a room at the library was also named in her honor.

When she retired in 1985, she had served as the city's librarian for forty-four years and had been a local historian for some fifty years. Her plan for retirement was to put all her news clippings, photos and notes together and

Above: Naomi Alice Gibbing, who served as librarian at Utica Public Library from 1941 to 1985. Gibbing was from a pioneer Utica family that settled in the area in 1831, and she was regarded as the unofficial historian of Utica. *From the* Macomb Daily.

Left: Naomi Gibbing was the Utica librarian for forty-four years. *Courtesy of the Utica Heritage Association.*

publish a book. While the project was well on its way, she passed away at the age of eighty-one in 1998 before finishing the work.

In her will, Gibbing asked her friend of forty years and fellow history buff JoAnn Burgess to take charge of her writings and finish compiling them into a manuscript for publication. Burgess and a committee from the city's Heritage Association that included R. Bruce Fisher III, Marvin C. Stadler, Jaqueline Noonan, Pat Hallman and Gloria Grove Olman, completed the task. A retired journalism instructor, Olman is credited with doing the bulk of the work on the book, including collecting photos, conducting interviews and writing additional pages beyond what Gibbing had completed.

It took six years of devotion to the project, and the book, *A History of Utica, Michigan*, was published in 2010. The 288-page hardcover book, complete with stories and photographs, both black and white and color, is now safely tucked in on a shelf at Gibbing's beloved city library.

13

Warren

As the largest city in Macomb County and the third-largest city in the state, Warren has certainly come a long way from when it was simply swampland and farms known as Beebe's Corners. Settled in 1830 by John L. Beebe, who ran the toll booth at Chicago and Mound, the city was later named after war hero Reverend Abel Warren. The city continued to grow, but during the Depression, building and expansion stopped until President Franklin D. Roosevelt devised programs to help. In 1940, during World War II, the Detroit Tank Arsenal became the first manufacturing plant to mass-produce tanks in the United States. After the arsenal was built, many jobs began opening at the GM Tech Center. In 1957, Warren was incorporated as a city—prosperity had arrived. Today, the city boasts a population over 135,000 and covers thirty-four square miles.

GOVERNOR ALEXANDER JOSEPH GROESBECK

Homegrown in Macomb

He didn't campaign by handing out literature, kissing babies or even shaking hands. Instead, Alexander Groesbeck remained calm and self-contained while being bold, straightforward and eager to tackle tough issues. His lack of a back-slapping political pose made some citizens uncomfortable, thinking he was cold or indifferent, but style aside, he was certainly an important part of Michigan politics in the 1920s and beyond.

The thirtieth governor of Michigan was born on a farm in Warren Township in 1873, one of six children of Macomb County sheriff Louis Groesbeck and his wife, Julia (Coquillard) Groesbeck. When Louis was elected Macomb County Sheriff in 1880, the family had to move to Mount Clemens. At that time, the sheriff and his family lived at the jail, which had two stories and a basement. The main floor was the sheriff's office, sitting room, bedroom and a parlor, while the second floor had four rooms, a closet and a restroom. The basement had two cellars, one bedroom, a kitchen and a dining room. Nearby was the three-story jail with eighteen cells and dimensions of thirty feet by thirty-two feet. Sheriff Groesbeck and family were the first to occupy the new living quarters, and it was there that Alex Groesbeck was inspired to follow a profession in law. He spent many hours reading over government reports and papers on civil and criminal practices, and having a paper route kept him appraised of all the latest local news. He lived in Wallaceburg, Ohio, for several years and when the family returned to Michigan, he went to work in his father's sawmill until he was seventeen and the lumber business in Michigan went into decline. Determined to get a good education, Groesbeck did a variety of odd jobs, including studying the law in the offices of some local attorneys, looking forward to going to law school himself.

He entered law school at the University of Michigan in 1892, graduated a year later and went into private practice in Detroit, where he was quickly recognized for his hard work and professionalism. Groesbeck entered state politics in 1912 when he led a delegation to the Republican National Convention to renominate President Howard Taft. He was also elected as state party chairman and retained the post until 1914. He was a candidate for governor in 1914 but lost that bid at the state's top office. In 1916, he was elected to a two-year term as attorney general of Michigan and won another term in 1918. In 1920, he won the Republican primary election for governor, defeating Democrat and former governor Woodbridge N. Ferris. Groesbeck was elected two more times, serving a total of six years as the head of the state. During his tenure as governor, he was a strong supporter for revamping major roads in Michigan and at one point, his campaign slogan was "Take Michigan out of the Mud." He also advocated for school choice, prison reform and government consolidation.

Prior to 1920, most Michigan roads were simply dirt and gravel, and became impassable in the spring due to rain and cold temperatures.

Governor Alexander Groesbeck. *Courtesy of the Warren Historical and Genealogical Society.*

Funded by private companies who wanted people to buy more cars and auto parts, Groesbeck found that approach ineffective and instituted a two-cents-per-gallon gas tax. He also added an automobile tax based on weight, not horsepower, claiming roads should be funded by those who use them. Noting that gravel and asphalt were highly inferior products, Groesbeck saw Michigan become the first to utilize concrete. He also moved three cemeteries to see Woodward Avenue extended so that it connected Detroit to Pontiac and used convict labor to build the highways.

Beyond roads, schools of choice became another major issue when Groesbeck was governor. Michigan was one of the first states to establish public schools, but private schools continued to exist. Many parents paid tax dollars to public schools and tuition for a private school. In 1920, however, the public-school lobby placed an amendment on the ballot to abolish private schools. The amendment would mandate a public-school education for all children in Michigan. Campaigning for governor, Groesbeck denounced this proposal as a violation of the First Amendment to the U.S. Constitution and urged the Supreme Court of Michigan to take the proposal off the ballot. The court refused Groesbeck's request, but the voters elected him governor for a second term. The school choice issue came up again in 1924 during Groesbeck's campaign for a third two-year term. The Ku Klux Klan had gathered strength in Michigan and endorsed the effort to ban private schools. The Klan also tried to unseat Groesbeck in the primary by backing James Hamilton, a Canadian-born miner and longshoreman. Groesbeck did not back down and campaigned vigorously for tolerance, individual liberty and school choice while denouncing the Klan. Beating his opponent by more than two to one, Groesbeck retained the governorship and stunned the Democrats.

During his three terms as governor, Groesbeck was seen as a dictator at times and disinterested in reaching out to his constituents on any personal level. His time in the governor's office saw advancement in the state's highway system and also in prison reform measures, plus an automobile title system was created and the state government was restructured and consolidated. Groesbeck was stymied in a quest to get a fourth term in office, defeated in the Republican primary in 1926 by Fred W. Green.

Groesbeck never cared for dancing or social engagements, and he remained a bachelor. He made lots of money over the years and made more in Detroit's growing real estate market, buying property whenever and wherever he could. A large house downtown he purchased for himself and his sister soon seemed to be too much, and Groesbeck thought it was unjust and even unwise to maintain a house that was half empty. So, he had the mansion divided up into apartments and invited the public in keeping a smaller bachelor quarters for himself and room for his sister. He remained involved in business and legal activities but still had energy to burn in recreational pastimes. Groesbeck was reputed to be an excellent boxer and wrestler in businessmen's athletic-club circles.

In 1953, Groesbeck died at the age eighty from congestive heart failure. As flags across the state were ordered flown at half-staff, Governor G. Mennen Williams said the state had lost a true elder statesman and his predecessor's death gave the current generation cause to remember that greatness is not an accident but flows from the wisdom and leadership of ᵗen like Alexander J. Groesbeck.

MAYOR TED BATES

A Tenacious, Honest Leader

When you're a politician and you make yourself available to your constituents around the clock, it breeds appreciation but can also lead to burnout. For the fourteen years Warren mayor Ted Bates served in the city's top spot, from 1967 to 1981, residents used to call him at home at all hours. One evening, he had just gotten home after spending hours hauling buckets of water following a citywide flood and was literally sleeping at the kitchen table, and the phone just kept ringing with angry callers. He finally had to get a private phone number. Still, it didn't stop him from answering concerns with his usual personal style. Many residents said he always dealt with things head on, not hiding behind his title or his office door. Bates once said his own political philosophy was simple, if he could do something for someone he would; if he couldn't, he would admit it wasn't possible.

Born in Detroit in 1926 to James and Nina Bates, Ted Bates was just seventeen during World War II, and he followed his three brothers into the navy, dropping out of high school to do so. Bates attained the rank of seaman first class. When he returned, he finished school, and in 1948, when he was working in accounting with Detroit's Mistle Coal & Coke, Ted married Eleanor Puzzoll. He became a volunteer fireman in Warren and soon began working at the city administration offices. He spent six years as an assistant to Warren's first mayor, Arthur Miller, who was elected in 1957. In 1961, Bates was elected city treasurer and, in 1967, to the mayor's office himself. It was a tumultuous time in the city, with flooding and a garbage strike, and riots broke out in the nearby city of Detroit that summer.

In April 1968, the city launched a Crime Commission with twelve individuals appointed by Mayor Bates to investigate the crime situation and draw up programs with citizens' cooperation. At that time, gun sales were soaring, and people were stockpiling food and supplies. A local newspaper reported that Bates wanted to alleviate citizen concerns, and he assured them there was no need to turn their homes into arsenals. The city had hired sixty-one new police officers, the highest number in the ranks in the city's history.

The mayor's office made headlines in 1970 when Bates demanded a public apology from Secretary of Housing and Urban Development George Romney after Romney told a Senate committee that Warren had an obvious policy in place for housing discrimination. Bates took offense to the comments and stated that the city was not preventing anyone from moving in, and in fact, they weren't breaking any laws and weren't discriminating against anyone. Romney threatened to withhold $2.8 million in Housing and Urban Development (HUD) funding to the city until Warren set up a human relations committee to deal with open housing opportunities. Bates said he felt HUD was trying to use Warren to establish forced integration on the city; Romney denied it. Bates pushed the city into the national spotlight a second time when he opposed cross-district busing.

Mayor Ted Bates. *From the* Macomb Daily.

Another big headline in 1973 regarding the Bates administration came when the city council voted to double the salaries of all its administrators. Bates had been making $14,000, and the increase paid him $29,000. At the time, elected officials in city hadn't had raises for fifteen years, and Bates stated the seventy city employees were making more than him and it was ridiculous.

Outspoken but hands on, Bates grabbed a shovel during a garbage strike to help out, drove an amphibious vehicle during the city floods, once chased a hit-and-run driver on foot for nearly a mile and wasn't above standing in the lobby at city hall with his eyes on the clock as employees arrived for work just to keep everyone on their toes. When the city completed work on a $27 million sewage treatment plant, Bates was so proud he invited reporters to take a swim and said he'd take a drink of water from the tank if they wanted him to. All this occurred while the city's population nearly tripled during his tenure.

A family man who still lived in the same house where he and his wife, Eleanor, raised their five children, Bates was fortunate to have a spouse who put as much into the city as he did. Supporting her husband during fourteen years in the mayor's office, Eleanor Bates was referred to as the first lady of Warren for years beyond his tenure there. She later served on Warren City Council, Warren Community Development Corporation, the Warren Beautification Commission, Warren Symphony Board, Warren Concert Band Board and the Warren Historical Society. She remains a member of the Lincoln High School Alumni Association and was elected to the Board of Education in June of 2005.

When Bates suffered a heart attack a decade into his time in the mayor's office in 1977, there was a bit of a skirmish between him and Mayor Pro Tem George Dimas, who questioned his fitness for office. Dimas requested a full medical report on the mayor's condition and stated he was ready to take over running the city. Bates press secretary Jack Combs quickly assured all those concerned the mayor was running the city from his bedside and all was fine, stating nothing had happened to his head. He had other critics from time to time too. In 1979, when council members Lillian Dannis and Carmella Sabaugh, who often sided against the mayor on issues, were elected to the treasurer and clerk's offices, it was an upset for the mayor. As the departments butted heads, the ladies soon found themselves without the courtesy of city cars normally allotted to city department heads.

In 1981, Bates faced a challenge for the mayor's office when, for the third time, Jim Randlett, a police officer in the city, challenged him at the polls. Bates had a $30,000 campaign war chest, employees willing to take vacation days to campaign for him and three hundred volunteers on the campaign trail too. At that time, the mayor's salary was $35,000 a year, with perks like a car, insurance, an expense account and three full-time administrative assistants, called secretaries then. Despite all that positive reinforcement, Randlett beat Bates by just 1,109 votes in a harsh campaign that saw the president of the city's International Association of Fire Fighters arrested for trying to sell his union's endorsement of Bates for $1,000. Bates challenged Randlett and his team to take lie detector tests to see if they were involved in trying to bribe the same fire official.

His administration's good works remained in Warren, from the Waste Water Treatment Plant, the 37th District Court complex, several libraries, fire stations and an impressive police station. A city park on Warkop, south of 14 Mile and east of Van Dyke, is named in his honor.

In 1982, under the guise of not forgetting all he did for the city, his friends hosted a $100 a plate dinner in Bates's honor at his favorite restaurant in the city, Tutag's on the Hill, where 175 people showed up. Some thought it might be funding for another run at the city's top office, but Bates assured them his political life was behind him. He took a job at GM, retired from there in 1992 and moved to northern Michigan with his second wife.

Bates died in 2011 at the age of eighty-four after suffering a heart attack at his northern Michigan chalet. He was survived by five children and several grandchildren. Local politicians who recalled his reign in the city said he was a straight shooter, honest and spoke from the heart. Richard Sabaugh, who served on the Macomb County Board of Commissioners remembered Bates this way:

> *He was straightforward and always honest. You could never accuse him of being deceptive. What you saw was what you got. He left a legacy of hard work. Bates was the symbol of city government. He was always the first one there in the morning and the last one to leave at night.*

ARTHUR AND EDNA MILLER

Sad Circumstances Created Miller Dynasty

They married young, had six children and shared a devotion to public service—even if Edna Miller's introduction to office came about following the untimely death of her husband, Arthur Miller, at the age of forty-two. Much to the surprise of many, Edna Miller was appointed to fill the remaining term her husband had been serving as the Macomb County clerk, and she went on to retain the seat for a record twenty-eight years.

Arthur Miller began his political career in 1945 at the age of twenty-one when he was elected justice of the peace in Warren Township. Two years later, he was elected township supervisor and then served four consecutive terms in that spot. While he was in office, the township became the City of Warren, and he became the city's first mayor, a seat he filled until 1960. As the township and then city struggled to establish itself, Miller was involved in many issues, from flooding problems, the construction of apartments to accommodate employees at the GM Tech Center and other new development coming to town during tough financial times.

In the summer of 1957, horrendous floods filled streets and basements in the city. Miller had movies made to try to garner attention for the problem and bring about funding for storm relief projects. The films were sent to the Macomb–Oakland County Drain Commission, which was considering a $1.5 million project for Bear Creek Drain in Warren. In 1958, he was part of contingent of local politicians and community supporters who welcomed the development of Lorraine Manor, a fifty-eight-unit apartment complex, state of the art for its time with multiple bedroom units all with air conditioning with rent between $105 to $130 a month. Miller was also leading the city when General Motors agreed to purchase 123 acres with sixteen buildings

Arthur J. Miller, who took office as the first mayor of the city of Warren on January 1, 1967. He also served as Macomb County clerk from 1960 until his death in 1964. This view shows him at his desk while mayor of Warren. *From the* Macomb Daily.

that formerly belonged to the Naval Industrial Reserve at Nine Mile and Mound for $3.5 million. The property hadn't been in use for more than two years, and Miller hailed the deal as a boon to the city.

It seems Miller's time in office met with regular pushback from at least one member of the city council. On one occasion, Councilman Irvin G. Little referred to Miller as "acting like a Gestapo," while Miller countered with a claim that Little was playing politics. The row came about because Miller blanched at giving the police officers a $350 raise and instead favored a $150 increase. Another time, Little was recording city council meetings and Miller objected, stating he didn't want his voice recorded and said he would have the outlet in the wall removed for the next meeting if Little persisted. Ultimately, the council voted 5–4 to allow the recordings to continue.

Beyond his office, Miller was hospitalized for six weeks in 1959 after suffering a heart attack. He spent two more weeks in the hospital in 1960 after being diagnosed with a racing heart, but he said it was not another heart attack. In 1960, Miller was elected as Macomb County clerk and was reelected in 1962 on the Democratic ticket. He was on a business trip to Hawaii in 1964 when he suffered a fatal heart attack. He and Macomb County drain commissioner Thomas Welsh were delegates from the Huron-Clinton Metropolitan Authority attending a conference on recreation development. County prosecutor George Parrish said Miller's death was a great loss to him personally, and the county family and the county had lost a very good official.

When Edna Miller agreed to take a seat as the clerk in Macomb County after the loss of her husband, it was a pioneering move—the 1960s, wives and mothers weren't expected to join the workforce and particularly not politics. Her son Arthur Miller Jr. recalled people were not shy about stating that she should be at home with her children and there was no place for her in politics. He said his mother simply explained to him and his siblings that they are not quitters and their father would want them to move forward. In 1964, a panel of county judges appointed Edna Miller to serve out her husband's term, and two years later she ran and won her first election. An admired and well-respected administrator, she ran successful reelection campaigns for another two decades and always remained well ahead of any challengers.

Edna Mae Miller. When her husband, Arthur J. Miller Sr., died suddenly in 1964, she was appointed by a panel of judges to fill his unexpired term as Macomb County clerk and held the position for twenty-eight years. *From the Macomb Daily.*

The most memorable challenge came in 1992: Edna Miller drew criticism when she decided to collect her pension without retiring. Macomb County was the only place in the state where that was allowed, and it was later revoked by new legislation. She was challenged in the August primary by Warren city clerk and Democrat Carmella Sabaugh, who called the pension a double dip and even sent out campaign literature depicting an ice cream cone with two scoops. The tactic worked, and Miller was ousted after serving a total of twenty-eight years in the clerk's office.

Still, along the way, the family political gene soared. Art Miller Jr. served in the Michigan Senate from 1977 to 2003, where he was a strong Democratic leader for twenty-five years. His brother Thomas Miller was named chairman of the Macomb Community College Board of Trustees. The third generation of Miller politicians came via grandson Derek Miller, son of Arthur Miller Jr., who was elected to a term in the Michigan House of Representatives, served as treasurer of Macomb County and worked as an assistant prosecutor.

Edna Miller was suffering from colon cancer when she passed away in 1996 at the age of seventy-three. She left an impressive legacy, dubbed a trailblazer for women in county politics, paving the way for what has become a very large field of women in politics in Macomb County. Sheriff William Hackel said Miller was a strong lady; not much rattled her, and she reminded him of former first lady Barbara Bush, dignified and down-to-earth. She also managed to always put family first.

14

Washington Township

The land that makes up Washington Township was first surveyed in 1818, but the official meeting to organize the township wasn't held until 1827. When it came time to deciding on a name, resident Daniel Thurston suggested the township be named after the father of our country, and Washington was enthusiastically accepted by the group. The township originally included what is today Washington and Bruce Townships. Bruce Township became a separate entity in 1833. By 1850, Washington Township had 119 farms, and just twenty-four years later, that number had grown to 196. A significant part of the farming history of the area is related to the beautiful orchards that have been there over decades, although just four remain today. The township has a population of twenty-four thousand and covers thirty-six square miles.

WILLIAM AUSTIN BURT

A Pioneer, Inventor and Public Servant

A man with endless ideas, William Austin Burt, referred to in history annals as the "father of the typewriter," sometimes found his inventions were before their time, He was born in Massachusetts in 1792 and took an interest in mathematics, astronomy and philosophy from an early age. He also

William Austin Burt. *Courtesy of the Utica Heritage Association.*

developed great mechanical skills. When he was eighteen, he purchased a broken surveying compass, repaired it and surveyed the area near his home; it was a precursor to what was to come. Burt enlisted in the U.S. Army in 1812 and then married Phoebe Cole in 1813. While in Wales Center in Erie County, New York, Burt served as the justice of the peace, postmaster and county surveyor. Over the next five years, with his eye on becoming a U.S. deputy surveyor, Burt traveled the country as a millwright.

In 1822, he settled in the village of Mount Vernon, north of Detroit, which later became Washington Township. Burt worked as surveyor, and in 1829, he invented a small wooden box with a swinging lever that he could depress to make an impression. The lever was attached to a short sector beneath it, and letters could be imprinted in upper and lower case on a sheet of rolled paper, like that of a paper towel dispenser. The paper was then torn off to be used. Burt received a patent in 1829, signed by President Andrew Jackson, and it was good for fourteen years. Sadly, Burt's typewriter/typographer was ahead of its time, and despite his creation of another model a few months later, there was no market for the product.

In 1833, Burt was appointed a U.S. deputy surveyor. At that time, three of his sons, John, Alvin and Austin, were old enough to work as assistant surveyors to learn the trade. In the next eighteen years, his five sons, including

Wells and William, became U.S. deputy surveyors too. He also trained many other young men as surveyors over the years.

Amid his work for the U.S. government, Burt continued to be creative in his home workshop, and in 1835 he invented and patented a solar compass for surveyors. The solar compass, much more precise than magnetic models, was very well received and brought national attention to Burt as a top surveyor. His was a prototype for the ones still in use today.

As a surveyor, Burt took ten years to record Michigan's Upper Peninsula and was credited with discovering the first iron ore in Marquette County. Burt later became a surveyor for Macomb County and, throughout his life, was a millwright and held public offices, including county surveyor.

A Jefferson Democrat, Burt wasn't really active politically, but he was a member and later named a judge of the Michigan Territorial Council. He served as the first postmaster for Mount Vernon in 1832, was a Macomb County circuit court judge in 1833 and a state legislator in 1853. Still, his greatest achievement was likely his time as a U.S. surveyor, which lasted from 1833 to 1853.

Burt moved to Detroit in 1857 and died the next year at the age of sixty-six. His great grandson Austin built a working model of the typographer for the 1893 Chicago's World Columbian Exposition and displayed it. The model is now housed in the Smithsonian Institution in Washington, D.C. The letter displayed next to the typewriter was written in 1830 by Burt to his wife, whom he addressed as "Dear Companion."

A site was dedicated in Burt's name by the State of Michigan in Stoney Creek Metropolitan Park sponsored by the Greater Washington Area Historical Society on September 21, 1986. Present at the dedication ceremony were three great-great-great-grandsons of William Austin Burt: John Burt, Richard Burt and James Burt.

John Dyer-Hurdon

This Leader Was Always Prepared

When he was just a boy, bored trying to get attention from his mother who was busy with his two sisters, John Dyer-Hurdon went to a meeting of the local Boy Scouts. Just one gathering back in 1942, and the young Dyer-Hurdon was hooked. He loved the activities and the camaraderie so much he spent the rest of his life bringing hundreds if not thousands of boys into the fold.

Logging a stunning seventy-five years in scouting, the breadth of his work came to life in Washington Township in 1985 when they opened the first museum in southeast Michigan totally devoted to the history of the Boy Scouts and Girl Scouts. Occupying a huge room in the old Washington High School that also houses the Washington Historical Museum, under the direction of Dyer-Hurdon, the museum thrived, displaying hundreds of items from his personal collection, his life in scouting proudly on display.

Scouting originated in England when Sir Robert Baden-Powell organized a camp for twenty boys in 1907. He did so upon discovering that many military troops had grown up in cities without any knowledge of survival in the wilderness. The movement was brought to the United States by a Chicago newspaper publisher, William D. Boyce, in 1910.

It was a Troop 246 meeting at the Calvin United Presbyterian Church in Detroit that captured Dyer-Hurdon's attention as a youth, and he remained a member of the troop until he earned Eagle Scout status in 1946. It quickly became obvious that he found his calling, as he was also a junior assistant

John Dyer-Hurdon (*left*) was part of the Boy Scouts of American for an impressive seventy-five years. *Courtesy of the Dyer-Hurdon family.*

Scoutmaster and Den Chief for Cub Scout Pack 246 and soon joined the Sea Scout Explorers, which introduced water-based adventures and career paths for youths.

Around that same time, Dyer-Hurdon was asked to join the Order of the Arrow, which is the National Honor Society for Scouting, and he was actually inducted into it before it was officially a Boy Scouts of America program. Around this time, in 1948, Dyer-Hurdon put on a new uniform after enlisting in the U.S. Naval Reserves and the U.S. Navy. He signed on for a three-year tour, but that was extended because of the Korean War, and he served over four years total, including two and a half years in a submarine.

He married Dolores Foster in 1950, and they had three children: John in 1956, Heather in 1958 and James in 1961. While he remained active in the Sea Scout Explorers, Dyer-Hurdon organized Boy Scout Troop 156 in 1968 with just five boys at Peach Lutheran Church in Shelby Township. He emphasized Americanism and good citizenship from the very beginning and attended summer camp (one week) every year with the troop. During his tenure as scoutmaster, sixty scouts earned the Eagle Award. He had, at times, eighty-seven active boys registered in Troop 156.

When Dyer-Hurdon retired as Scoutmaster of Troop 156 in 1985, after serving in that position for seven years, he reorganized Cub Scout Pack 77 and served as assistant Cubmaster for two years. During this time, the Pack grew to 130 active Cub Scouts. He served as Cubmaster for a few years and then organized a Weblos Den called 10 Little Indians but soon had 15 Weblos, including his grandson. In 2007, Clinton Valley Council created the Jack Dyer-Hurdon Weblos Transition Award (shoulder patch). It is given to leaders and Cub Scouts whose dens transition to a scout troop from Weblos.

Looking back, Dyer-Hurdon's daughter Heather Gibbs said their family lived, slept and ate scouting. Both of her brothers attained Eagle Scout status, while she attained the highest award in Camp Fire Girls. Scouting was a way of life for the family, and even when she wasn't an official part of the troop, she attended all the functions. She recalled her father being busy thirty-five weekends a year with scouting, and he even put his own artistic talents into it. Calling him "a phenomenal artist and woodworker," Gibbs recalled the times he made many clay models for the scouting program and the time he brought a pair of telephone poles into their basement and turned them into totem poles.

Beyond scouting, Dyer-Hurdon, who spent his career as a mold maker at the GM Tech Center in Warren, started the Shelby Township cleanup program and was a member of the VFW Old Settlers Post 4629 as well

Portrait of John Dyer-Hurdon in Washington Township. *Courtesy of the Dyer-Hurdon family.*

as the Scottish Military Society. He was also an avid environmentalist and conservationist, and in 1973, he was awarded a certificate from the National Wildlife Federation for a backyard wildlife habitat.

Despite his artistic talents, leadership ability and attention to the environment, Dyer-Hurdon's legacy is best represented at the museum he created in Washington Township. Until his death in 2017 at the age of eighty-six, he was the one giving tours and taking groups of Cub Scouts, Boy Scouts, Explorers and Girl Scouts through the museum. By 2004, the museum had welcomed ten thousand visitors, and adding another fifteen years, up to today, it's likely exceeded twenty-five thousand tours.

The museum boosts several collections, among them are Boy and Girl Scout uniforms, equipment and patches dating back to 1924; Explorer uniforms and equipment; Sea Scouting memorabilia; and Camp Fire Girls (now called CampFire Girls and Boys). Donating much of the museum's memorabilia, either from his own collection or via donations he received over the years, Dyer-Hurdon even gave his collection of 240 coffee mugs to the museum. Other items of interest include cook kits, canteens, pup tents, flag kits, camp blankets from the 1920s and one of the rarer pieces in the collection, a complete Air Scout uniform from the 1940s.

Gibbs recently paid a visit to the museum, something she hadn't been able to bring herself to do since her father's passing. She felt a rush of emotions, pride for his work and sorrow at his loss but mostly a deep admiration and respect for the man who changed the course of so many boys' lives simply because he was a good guy.

About the Author

A local weekly newspaper in Macomb County gave Barb Pert Templeton her start as a professional journalist. Bylines in the *Detroit Free Press*, the *Observer* and *Eccentric Newspapers* and several national publications followed, along with articles for *Metro Parent* and *Macomb Now* magazines. But it was telling the stories from the local small towns via *The Voice* and its sister paper, the *Macomb Daily*, that captured her attention. Sharing a closer look at the personalities of the county she grew up in has been interesting and exciting, as she strives to find those stories from the past that have been overlooked up to now.